1,000,000 Books

are available to read at

www.ForgottenBooks.com

Read online
Download PDF
Purchase in print

ISBN 978-1-331-60884-4
PIBN 10212360

This book is a reproduction of an important historical work. Forgotten Books uses state-of-the-art technology to digitally reconstruct the work, preserving the original format whilst repairing imperfections present in the aged copy. In rare cases, an imperfection in the original, such as a blemish or missing page, may be replicated in our edition. We do, however, repair the vast majority of imperfections successfully; any imperfections that remain are intentionally left to preserve the state of such historical works.

Forgotten Books is a registered trademark of FB &c Ltd.
Copyright © 2018 FB &c Ltd.
FB &c Ltd, Dalton House, 60 Windsor Avenue, London, SW19 2RR.
Company number 08720141. Registered in England and Wales.

For support please visit www.forgottenbooks.com

1 MONTH OF FREE READING

at

www.ForgottenBooks.com

By purchasing this book you are eligible for one month membership to ForgottenBooks.com, giving you unlimited access to our entire collection of over 1,000,000 titles via our web site and mobile apps.

To claim your free month visit:

www.forgottenbooks.com/free212360

* Offer is valid for 45 days from date of purchase. Terms and conditions apply.

English
Français
Deutsche
Italiano
Español
Português

www.forgottenbooks.com

Mythology Photography **Fiction** Fishing Christianity **Art** Cooking Essays Buddhism Freemasonry Medicine **Biology** Music **Ancient Egypt** Evolution Carpentry Physics Dance Geology **Mathematics** Fitness Shakespeare **Folklore** Yoga Marketing **Confidence** Immortality Biographies Poetry **Psychology** Witchcraft Electronics Chemistry History **Law** Accounting **Philosophy** Anthropology Alchemy Drama Quantum Mechanics Atheism Sexual Health **Ancient History Entrepreneurship** Languages Sport Paleontology Needlework Islam **Metaphysics** Investment Archaeology Parenting Statistics Criminology **Motivational**

BEFORE THE FOOT-LIGHTS.

BY REV. F. M. IAMS,

AUTHOR OF

"BEHIND THE SCENES."

"THE TRUTH SHALL MAKE YOU FREE."—JESUS.

CINCINNATI, O.:
G. W. LASHER, PUBLISHER.
1885.

Entered according to Act of Congress, in the year 1884, by

F. M. IAMS,

In the Office of the Librarian of Congress, at Washington.

PREFACE.

THIS book is intended as a sequel to *Behind the Scenes*. In that work the author gives the reader an idea of the severe struggles through which he became a Baptist. There the reader may watch certain processes of thought resulting in a firm conviction of the truth; here he may inspect a portion of the evidences on which that conviction rests. There he may dwell on some of the incidents of an earnest inquest after the old gospel practice; here he may see that practice accurately and distinctly mapped out by many of the most competent among those who refuse to observe it. There he may study a conflict of opinions; here he finds himself in an arsenal full of Baptist ammunition furnished by first-class pedobaptist factories.

It is a significant fact that the most eminent pedobaptist expositors and writers, in ever-growing numbers, are turning the shotted batteries of Divine Truth upon the citadels of pedobaptist errors. In these pages the writer would aid them in this good work, by combining many of those batteries in such way that they may deliver one tremendous, prolonged broadside against Sprinkling and Infant Baptism. Having great faith in the honesty of the masses of his pedobaptist brethren, he invites them to ponder the testimonies of scores of their very best writers, as set forth in these pages, in the confident hope that very many of them will do so, and that, doing so, they will discern and obey the truth.

Some of our good Baptist friends have an idea that many pedobaptists *are afraid to read up* on pedobaptist practices, and it must be owned that facts are not wanting to justify that idea, in very many instances. A good way to refute it would be to march boldly up to these FOOTLIGHTS, and read every page, and every paragraph, carefully and prayerfully. The author charges nothing for this suggestion, and ventures to hope that many will act upon it.

Trusting that this book may contribute, in some small degree at least, to the triumph of the truth, and to the unity and peace of the Churches of Christ, he sends it forth in the name of the Master, invoking his blessing upon all who may read it.

F. M. IAMS.

CONTENTS.

		PAGE
I.	The Real Issue,	7
II.	The Kingship of Christ,	30
III.	Sectarianism a Curse,	51
IV.	Testimony of the Lexicons,	68
V.	Concessions of Pedobaptist Writers,	87
VI.	Testimony of the Encyclopedias,	110
VII.	The Symbolism of Baptism,	127
VIII.	Infant Baptism,	153
IX.	History of Infant Baptism,	175
X.	More Witnesses,	200
XI.	Pedobaptist Defenses,	219
XII.	The Foot-lights Focalized,	239

BEFORE THE FOOT-LIGHTS.

I.

THE REAL ISSUE.

"Why not come back into your old church home?"
—An Old Friend.

My Dear Brother:—Your question attests your friendship, and therefore I have read it with great pleasure. It proves that your confidence in me is unchanged, and that our Christian fellowship still survives, in all its old-time vigor and sweetness, despite the sundering of our church relations, and I cherish it as a very precious memento. At the same time it touches the very core of all our differences, and challenges a candid consideration and a frank and courteous reply.

You are not mistaken in thinking that I still

have a very high regard for my pedobaptist brethren. The truth is that I love them very dearly. But when you ask, "Why not come back into your old church home?" truth obliges me to reply, I can not, for many good reasons. It is one thing to love the *good* in our brethren, but quite another thing to condone and fellowship the *bad* in their practices, by entering into church relations with them. I recognize their faith, commend their zeal, and glory in their "labors of love;" but from their heretical views and practices I am obliged to dissent, by many considerations, some of which I will cheerfully submit to your inspection.

But first permit me, my dear brother, to remind you that *the issue between Baptists and their opponents is one of Bible fact.* If it were a question of taste, or a matter of mere sentiment, as many good people imagine, we might well treat it as a small affair, turning from the discussion of it, as a matter of slight importance, or giving it up at once as a problem that never can be definitely settled.

The old saw, "There is no accounting for tastes," is as true among Christians as elsewhere. Tastes differ in all the churches quite as much and as unaccountably as in the camps of the "Philistines." One is fond of gay colors, another prefers more modest tints, and a third admires the "Quaker drab." Walking in flowery meadows, one is charmed by the delicate pansies, another is attracted by the sweet-scented clover blossoms, while others see greater beauty in flowers of a larger growth.

We may cultivate taste, but rarely, if ever, can we create it or radically change it. Topsy-like, it just grows, but whence, or how, or why, who can tell? It reaches out in this direction or in that like the ivy on the church wall, but unlike that docile plant, it resents the intervention of those who would direct it into new paths by the compulsion of reason or the strong hand of authority. And though we amuse ourselves by learned talks about the laws of taste, they are a mere figment of the imagination. It has no law but its own sweet will. It is itself a law to its victim. Like another "Old Man of the Sea," it rides, and whom it rides it rules.

Who cares to reason with a taste? A man may be wise as Solomon, vigorous as Peter, gentle and loving as John, or exact and logical as Paul; nay, he may combine all these grand qualities, and in every way he may be fully equipped for the contest, he may be the very embodiment of wit and wisdom, of piety and learning, but all in vain—one poor little taste will beat him every time.

Evidently, therefore, if the issue between Baptists and pedobaptists were one of mere taste or sentiment, it would endure forever. Those who admire sprinkling on æsthetic grounds, and practice it as "the more beautiful" way, would always continue to do so; and those who *feel* that infant baptism is a great privilege, and that the Church ought to be composed of believers and their children, would *feel* so to the end of the chapter. And on the other hand, those Baptists, if any, with whom immersion is a mere sentiment, could never be persuaded to give it up, no matter how convincing the evidence against it. Thence it would follow that there must ever be a wide, painful and destructive schism in the body of Christ; a schism at once without rational excuse, or reasonable hope of remedy; a schism that undeniably scandalizes our common Christianity, impedes the progress of the gospel, mars the unity and impairs the beauty and strength of the Church, and causes multitudes to continue in the darkness and guilt of unbelief; a schism that fatally antagonizes the prayer of our Lord that his people may all be one, by rending them into many; a schism that, resting upon likes and dislikes and mere arbitrary preferences, must be as permanent as its cause.

And you will agree, my brother, that a strong confirmation of this view is seen in the conduct of those who regard the issue as only an affair of personal taste or feeling. They are not open to conviction. Argument is lost upon them, not because they are not able to appreciate it and feel its force; nor because they are dishonest and repudiate their own convictions of right and of duty; nor because they do not love the truth for its own sake, and for Christ's sake; but simply because they regard this whole question, in all its parts, as a matter of personal preference, in which each one may rightfully consult his own convenience and pleasure. They do not think of it as a question of Bible fact, or as a matter involving Christian principle and allegiance to the authority of Christ. They do not realize the fact that Christ has spoken the decisive word in respect to it.

They have been told a thousand times by those in whom they confide as wise and pious teachers, that "the Master is silent about it, leaving each one to make his own choice;" and, believing it to be a matter of indifference to the dear Savior, they proceed to please themselves.

And as each one gratifies his own taste, he laughs at the protests of his neighbors, or resents them as an impertinence. For he looks upon every appeal to the Scriptures, and upon every argument professedly drawn from them, with suspicion, rejecting them without examination, as so many covert attempts to coërce his taste. He says he has just as much right as any one to consult his own tastes in these matters, and that is undeniably true. And so he settles down in his own chosen ways, perfectly satisfied and almost unchangeably fixed. It is with him a question of taste, and his tastes are not likely to change. If he chances to be in the right, it is well, for he will count one in behalf of truth, and that is something; but if he happens to be in the wrong, it is bad, indeed, for there he will almost certainly remain to the end—a pious, but incurable, devotee of error.

But convince him, first of all, that the issue is not one of taste, nor of sentiment, but of Bible-fact, of scriptural truth, of Christian principle, and, if he is a real Christian, he will hasten to investigate it prayerfully and thoroughly by a searching study of the Divine Word.

And herein, humanly speaking, lies our only

hope of the ultimate settlement of all the questions belonging to and growing out of this great controversy. The issue is not one of likes and dislikes, of mere personal convenience, of arbitrary custom, or of baseless fancies, but of plain, sober, get-at-able Bible fact. The law of Christ concerning it is written in his Word, not obscurely, but plainly. It is stated in terms distinct and unequivocal. The words employed are definite in their meaning, and their sense may be very easily ascertained, beyond any reasonable doubt, by all who earnestly desire to know the truth. The will of the Master, clearly and fully expressed in his own words, and in the words of his inspired apostles, is illustrated in his actions and in theirs. The words and the actions so perfectly correspond each with the other, that no one who attentively and prayerfully compares them can long remain in doubt respecting duty. The Master, baptized "into* the Jordan" (Mark i. 9), indicates clearly the act constituting baptism. His apostles, baptizing only those who profess faith in him, indicate with equal clearness the proper subjects of the ordinance. In this way, as by a series of plain, simple object lessons, the Scriptures set forth the truth so

---

*See Revised Version of 1881.

clearly that it may be readily and unerringly known by every earnest Christian. And this is only another way of saying that the Bible is a success—a true revelation—actually revealing that which it undertakes to reveal. Surely, my brother, this is not an extravagant statement. The Divine Word plainly describes all those specific acts of obedience and of duty which it specifically requires at our hands. Will any Christian dare to dispute this simple statement? If it be true, then that Word affords an infallible criterion by which every one may test the varying doctrines and practices challenging attention and acceptance. And the process is a very simple one—an honest and constant appeal to "the law and the testimony," with a settled, prayerful purpose to accept and obey whatever of truth and of duty they may enjoin or inculcate. And the results of such an appeal must be well-nigh uniform. Perhaps there may be here and there an exception, due to some unfortunate personal twist or defect. But the rule will ever be uniformity of results among the great mass of seekers after the truth; otherwise the Scriptures themselves are at fault. For if we admit that the Scriptures require baptism at our hands, as they certainly do, and yet claim that it is not so defined that we can decide definitely what it is, that we do not know, and that we never can determine in what action it consists, we shall find it very difficult to retain our confidence in them as the Word of God. A thousand questions will spring up in our hearts and a great host of insuperable difficulties will beset our path, confronting and confounding our faith in the Bible. If it be indeed a revelation of the Divine Will concerning us, why is it that it does not make our duty plain in those things which it requires us to do? Is it possible that inspiration can not define the act of baptism so that men may know just what it is? What sane man can for a moment believe a thing so absurd? But if inspiration can make it plain, why are we left in doubt about it? Can perpetual schisms and controversies among his disciples be pleasing to the Master? Has he purposely left this whole matter indefinite and obscure, that his people may be always divided about it? Nay, that can not be, for he earnestly prays that "they all may be one," and he evidently regards their oneness as the conclusive evidence of his Messiahship—"that the world may believe that thou hast sent me." How can there be oneness of his people, without oneness and distinctness in the revelation of his will concerning vital doctrines and practical duties? How can they agree respecting duties that are not defined in the Word? How can there be such convincing oneness in the absence of any determinate rule of duty?

Can it be just to charge us with some specific duty, and yet to leave that duty so indeterminate that no one can ever certainly know whether he has performed the thing required? A human government, treating its citizens or subjects thus, would richly merit and surely receive the condemnation and hearty execration of all mankind, as intolerably unjust. It would be denounced and overthrown as an insupportable tyranny. Is our Lord less considerate and just than weak, sinful men? Is he an unreasonable tyrant? Here is a solemn duty of some sort involving some action by way of obedience; but what is that action? Here is a revelation; it is our sole and supreme rule of doctrine and duty, and by it we are to be judged; but what does it reveal? If in matters of duty its meaning can not be known, then it is not a revelation from God. He is certainly able to express his own will clearly and definitely; and he is too just, and wise, and good to leave us in hopeless darkness respecting any duty enjoined upon us. He may not choose to tell us why it is commanded, or to explain all the far-reaching consequences of the conduct required. He may require this or that simply because it pleases him to do so; but though the reason for so doing may not be explained, the thing commanded will always be stated definitely and plainly, so that all may know precisely *what* they are required to do. Less than this no man dare affirm of God as a moral governor. And a careful study of the Scriptures will satisfy every candid mind that they always conform to this just principle.

My brother, *the Bible is not at fault.* It is not, as some of its enemies have said, "like a fiddle, on which you can play whatever tune you will." It is not responsible for the discords and divisions so rife in the Christian world. It utters no uncertain sound. In all matters of vital truth and practical duty, its voices are accordant and intelligible to all. If men do not hear them alike and understand them alike, the fault is in them, not in it. You agree that *outside the pages of inspiration there is no warrant for the existence of church or ordinance.* They then are creatures of the Divine Word, depending upon it for their being, and for their right to be. That word is at once their charter and their supreme law, fixing unchangeably the character of the Church, determining the elements that shall compose it and the ordinances that shall be observed by it, both in character and form. Aside from that word no church has any right to exist, nor aside from it has any man any right to baptize. Nor has the Church any right to be other than that word requires, in membership, or in doctrines and usages. And the same thing is true in respect to ordinances. As no man may of right baptize any one except by authority of the Divine Word, so may he not baptize *any others* than of the class indicated in that word as the scripturally qualified subjects of baptism, nor may he baptize those in *any other way* than that prescribed by that word.

This is too evident to require a single word of proof. And it is equally evident that, if all men had always consulted the Divine Word, and faithfully obeyed it in constituting churches and in administering ordinances, there would never have been any controversy about baptism, nor would the Church have been so rudely and fatally rent into a multitude of discordant, warring sects. All who are unwilling to impeach the Holy Scriptures, and attempt to cast the blame upon them, must accept this conclusion.

It may be unpalatable, as it must be sad to

all; but since the divisions exist, and since the Word of God can not be at fault, they are chargeable to Christian men.

My brother, it is plain that the Baptists and their opponents can not both be right. There is such an antagonism between them, that one or the other must be decidedly wrong. The Baptist regards the gospel church as a company of regenerate persons—baptized believers—holding Christ as their only lawgiver, maintaining the doctrines and observing the ordinances of the gospel in due order, while nearly all pedobaptists look upon the church as a mixed company, composed of believers and their children. The difference between these two views of the gospel church is immense. It is the difference between the Apostolic Church in Jerusalem—spiritual, fraternal, holy and humble—and the Romish Church of to-day—worldly, ambitious, proud and corrupt. The one loves and serves with the spirit of her dear Master; the other covets, and grasps, and rules with the greed and the sword of a cruel Cæsar. The one is in the world, but not of it; the other is in the world and of it—of it in spirit, in ambition, in craftiness, in policies, and very largely in methods and details of government.

I do not mean to say that all pedobaptist churches are Romish; but the pedobaptist idea of the church finds in the Romish Church its fullest and most consistent and logical embodiment. In many pedobaptist churches a most blessed spirit of evangelism holds their ideal of the church constantly in check and prevents the development of its legitimate results by a continued infusion of a living spirituality. But in the Church of Rome, in the Church of England, and in a large share of the Lutheran Churches of Germany and the United States, the pedobaptist ideal is fairly seen in its mature fruits. Between these and the Apostolic Church in Jerusalem, the contrast is broad, deep and painful; but the difference, vast as it is, is due chiefly to the introduction of infants and unconverted children into the membership. These, introduced in great numbers, in accordance with the pedobaptist idea that the church is to be composed of "believers and their children," and growing up unregenerate, speedily converted those churches into great organized sections of a wicked world.

Apostolic Jerusalem, or Papal Rome—which is scriptural? Apostolic Jerusalem, or rationalistic German Lutheranism, or Episcopal Church of England formalism—which of these, my brother, is the true type of the Gospel Church? The Baptist affirms that Apostolic Jerusalem is the true type. The pedobaptist so defines the church, that, if we accept his definition and obey it, we can never approximate that type. The issue is a very distinct one—an issue of fact, to be tested and settled by the Word of God.

Again: The Baptist deems believers—those who make a credible profession of faith in our Lord Jesus—the only proper subjects of baptism; but the pedobaptist insists that children and unconscious babes are also suitable subjects of the initial Christian ordinance. This is an issue of fact, to be tested by the Word of God alone. If that Word requires, or in any way justifies, their baptism, then let them be baptized, but not otherwise. Baptists affirm that the immersion of a professed believer, and that alone, is Bible baptism; but pedobaptists insist that sprinkling or pouring of children and infants, as well as of adult believers, is also scriptural baptism. Here, again, is an issue of fact. Is sprinkling baptism? Is pouring baptism? What is the testimony of the Scriptures about it? Do they command sprinkling or pouring as baptism? Do they contain examples of such baptism? If so, it can be easily shown; but if not, then that fact can be definitely ascertained.

For all these great issues are questions of Bible *fact;* not of my taste, or of yours; of my preference, or of yours; of my ideas of propriety or of convenience, or of yours. As our opinions, preferences, tastes, desires, or ideas of the fitness of things, could never constitute a sufficient warrant for baptizing in any way whatever, or for instituting a church of any sort, so they can not justify any modification, either of baptism or of the church, in our practice.

Now, my brother, I think you can fully understand those obstacles that forbid my return to the pedobaptist fold. They may be summed up in one sentence: *The Word of God is in my way.* The issue between us is an issue of fact —not of taste nor of sentiment; and the Word of God, the only rightful or safe umpire in the matter, is against you. If I should come back to you, then the Word of God would be against me, too, and I would soon feel myself obliged to change my base.

If the things that separate us were only matters of taste on my part, or questions of preference, or mere sentiment, I protest solemnly that I would not let them stand in the way one moment. If they were really things indifferent—mere forms that one might innocently accept or reject, such as this or that attitude in prayer, or the use of this or that liturgy, or none at all, in public worship, or the wearing of this or that sort of coat or gown in the sacred desk—then I would certainly say, Let each one consult his own taste in such matters. I will frankly admit that I prefer a black coat in the sacred desk; but if you were happier, or more eloquent in a white gown, why, then, I would insist on your right to wear it. I will go further: Rather than occasion schism in the Church of Christ, I would consent to eat eggs three times a day during Lent, and even for a month afterward. Yes, and that is not all. I would actually agree to eat fish during the same period, stipulating only that it should be well-cooked and properly seasoned.

This ought to convince you that I am not at all bigoted in matters of taste and sentiment; and it is my firm conviction that in such things Baptists generally are every whit as liberal as I am. But when it comes to matters of conscience, you will concede at once that we ought not to do wrong, even to secure a coveted good; and I think you will also admit that we ought not to do that which we firmly believe to be wrong, in order that good may come of it. Now, we Baptists regard the thorough, honest union of all Christians in a true, gospel church fellowship as a very great, and a very desirable good, and we are willing to do all we dare to bring it about; but we dare not do wrong to secure it. And, indeed, it can not be secured in that way, were we willing to do the wrong; for the resulting union would not be deep and real, but superficial, and, on our part, hypocritical. You would despise our treason to our convictions of right, and we would despise ourselves for our want of loyalty to the Word of God. There is the insuperable difficulty in the way of Baptists who would come to you. I know, my dear brother, that you desire a union of all Christians, including Baptists; but, really, I can think of only two ways in which such union can ever be secured.

The first and most obvious way, since Baptists are but a minority of the Christian world, is for you pedobaptists to convince us that our understanding of the Word of God, in the matters at issue between us, is wrong, and that your view of it is right. And if we really are mistaken about it, you surely ought to be able to convince us of that fact, for you have in your ranks hosts of talented and highly educated men, who certainly can so "put things" as to make the *true* appear the *better* reason. Besides, in dealing with myself and with the great mass of our Baptist ministers, you have two very great advantages.

We like to be popular, perhaps as well as other folks, and yours is the popular side. If you could only win us over to your views, people would no longer stigmatize us as "bigots," a title that *grinds;* but they would call us "good fellows," "large-hearted," "sensible," "liberal;" and we, like other men, relish commendation. Then, hold your ear close and I will whisper it: If you could make us see our way clear to be pedobaptists, many of us would be greatly benefited financially, for we would get larger salaries. Now understand me. Our people are not mean, nor stingy, but they are comparatively few and poor, and they are carrying on a vast work for Christ. Nor are our ministers mercenary above others, for they labor quite as ably and quite as faithfully as their pedobaptist ministerial neighbors, and generally for much less pay by way of salary. Now, my brother, you can very readily understand how a good man, badly pinched for means, might consent the more readily to abandon a bad cause for a better one, when the change, right in itself, is sure to replenish his flattened purse. So, if you are *right*, the advantage is all on your side, and you ought to succeed. But I confess this plan is a little risky. Sometimes your people, in trying to pull our people out, break in themselves and go clear under, just as the boys who go skating often get into the water while trying to get some unfortunate one out of it. An instance just in point occurs to me. A Baptist gentleman residing in a certain Western State, a man of note in the State, married an excellent Presbyterian lady. She was very anxious that her husband should become a member of her church, and often spoke to him about it. The Governor, who was a very wise, practical man, finally told her that he would leave the entire matter with her, on one condition, viz.: that she should make a thorough, prayerful study of the subject, until confident that she fully understood the teaching of the Word of God about it; and then if she would say that, in her judgment, the Word of God required him to go with her into the Presbyterian Church, he would do so at once. She accepted the condition joyfully, and at once entered heartily into the investigation of the subject. Some weeks afterward, she timidly said to her husband: "I have examined that matter very thoroughly, and I desire to be baptized, and to join the Baptist Church with you."

That is the great danger, my brother, in trying to win us over to your views. Those who attempt it are so apt to become Baptists themselves! The pedobaptist ice is pretty thin, and those who venture upon it are almost certain to break through into the baptismal font. Of course, that don't hurt them, but it mortifies you, and gives you pain. I therefore propose a better and more speedy way of effecting the desired union, viz.: that you pedobaptists come over to us.

And this proposition is worthy your prayerful consideration; for you all acknowledge that we are right in affirming that immersion is scriptural baptism, and that believers are scriptural subjects of baptism, and that believers are scripturally qualified, when baptized, for membership in the Church of Christ. You admit, also, that baptism is a public confession of Christ—putting on Christ before the world—and that his Supper properly belongs to such, and only such, as profess themselves to be his friends.

Thus you confess that all we affirm is true,

while you are by no means sure that the things we deny are true. We deny that sprinkling is baptism, that infants are scriptural subjects of baptism, and that they are scripturally qualified for membership in the church. Now, my brother, you know that you can not prove that sprinkling is scriptural baptism, and you confess that you have no scriptural precept or example to justify the baptism of infants. And hosts of pedobaptist churches reject infant membership as decidedly as we Baptists reject it. You can come to us without any sacrifice of principle, and without giving up so much as one iota of established truth.

In our Baptist Churches you will find, clearly held and duly honored, every truth and every practice that is undeniably right and scriptural —yourself being judge—while you will miss only those doubtful and troublesome opinions and practices which you will find it impossible to establish by the authority of the Word of God, and which many of your own people openly reject and contemn, if not with your connivance, at least, without your open, vigorous condemnation.

Now, is not this a fair proposition? And it is one that you can accept without any loss of self-respect, or the least degree of humiliation.

And I can assure you that it will greatly add to your comfort and Christian assurance to know that you have conformed your creed and your practice to the clearly-perceived will of the Master. You know I have tried it, and speak from experience. If you lament our separation, come to Christ's standard of doctrine and duty, and there you will find us, ready to greet you with a hearty fellowship in Christ. Yours for the truth, ———.

II.

THE KINGSHIP OF CHRIST.

" Ye call me Master and Lord; and ye say well, for so I am."—JESUS.

MY DEAR BROTHER—In the estimation of all true Baptists the Kingship of Christ is a vital fact. To them he is in very deed the King of Saints. They behold him on the throne, and hasten to "crown him Lord of all." They accept fully the declaration of the great apostle to the Gentiles, that "Christ is the Head of the Church," whence they conclude that he is her one supreme Lawgiver. Hence, his will is to them the end of all controversy. In the most practical way they call him "Master" and "Lord," by making his Word their highest rule of doctrine and of duty. With them his voice silences doubt, debate and dissent, for it is the voice of their King, and its utterance is the final word, from which there is no appeal.

Remembering his words, "One is your

Master, even Christ, and all ye are brethren," they insist upon an absolute equality of rights among brethren, and an absolute subjection of all to that one Master. Their churches, consequently, are in themselves so many simple democracies, in which all the members have equal rights; but, considered in its relation to our Lord, each of those churches is a pure Christocracy, knowing no law and, in matters of faith and practice, confessing allegiance to no authority but that of Christ alone. The Holy Scriptures are the one "Book of Discipline" in all those churches, and the will of the Lord therein recorded is their unchangeable law.

In every case of doubt or of disagreement about any matter of doctrine or of practice, all true Baptists appeal not to the Fathers, nor to tradition, nor to councils, nor to musty terms of theological speculation, nor yet to the popular preferences and tastes of the masses, but to "the law and the testimony," believing very firmly that "if they speak not according to this Word, it is because there is no light in them." And this loyalty to Christ as King, manifesting itself in a constant and unswerving obedience to his will as revealed in his Written Word, is the real source of all the peculiarities observable among Baptists. The average Baptists have no natural partiality for immersion. If it were left to their choice, as a matter of taste or of convenience, they would be quite as apt as any others to adopt sprinkling, and discontinue the use of immersion altogether. Nor would they adhere to immersion because of any notion of a superior efficacy in the bath, for they do not believe there is one particle of virtue in water, no matter how it be used, nor whether the quantity employed be little or much, to cleanse the soul from the pollution of sin. Their only hope of such cleansing is not in the baptismal water, but in the atoning blood of Jesus, which alone, when accepted in true penitence and faith, is able to cleanse the soul from all unrighteousness.

But Jesus has commanded immersion, and Jesus is King, and true Baptists have no choice in the matter—an authority which they dare not disobey has fully determined it. And the same thing is true of all their other peculiarities. They adhere to them simply because loyalty to the King requires it. Take infant baptism. Who will pretend that Baptists do not love the little ones quite as well as do other people? Who will rise up and say that Baptist parents, as a class, are one whit less loving and affectionate toward their babes than other

Christian parents? Why, then, do they refuse baptism to their little ones? Simply because the King did not provide it for them, but only for such as consciously receive him, and intelligently believe in him. If he had said, "Baptize the babes," then they would hasten to do it, no matter what objections might be urged against it, for the command of the King is all the warrant they require for any practice that may challenge acceptance. With them Christ's prerogative is indisputable. In everything it is his to command, and ours unhesitatingly to hear and obey.

Thus the Kingship of Christ is the formative—the fundamental idea among Baptists. It controls them everywhere and always, determining their beliefs and their practices from first to last. Their rejection of sprinkling, and their faithful adherence to the practice of immersion, are due to this idea alone. So, too, their practice of believer's baptism only, and their persistent rejection of the baptism of infants, are due to the same fundamental principle. And in like manner their most offensive usage, the practice of restricted communion, is due to the same controlling idea—the practical recognition of the Kingship of our Lord in everything relating to his people and to his house. For his authority is as complete in the order of the ordinances as in any principle or precept of his gospel, and we may not set it aside.

Now, my dear brother, incredible as it may seem to you, this practical recognition of the Kingship of Christ is really the most vital of all the matters at issue between Baptists and pedobaptists. Theoretically all who call themselves Christians confess that Christ is King. But theory is one thing, and far too often practice is another and widely different thing. Theoretically our pedobaptist friends say Christ is King, and almost constantly they sing, "Crown him Lord of all;" but practically they reject his Kingly authority in the matter of baptism, and instead of rendering a joyful and implicit obedience to his command, they change that command to suit their own tastes, and then calmly tell us that their new way will do as well. Does this seem a grave charge against a vast body of the professed disciples of our Lord, and one that ought not lightly to be made? Well, I admit it. It is a grave charge, but it is as true as it is grave, and the evidences of its truth abound on every side. The current defense of sprinkling, viz.: that it will do as well as immersion, deliberately sets aside the Kingship of Christ. It assumes as true that which the pedobaptists of this age almost universally concede—that the Lord commands immersion—and assures us that a something else, which he does not command, will answer just as well. In other words, it weighs the command of our Lord in the scales of its own petty, human reason, and dares to set it aside, and to substitute for it a something different, which it pronounces just as good. If this is not a practical rejection of the Kingship of our Lord, what is it?

Suppose the Czar of Russia should issue a decree that every soldier in the Russian army be clothed in a uniform of blue, trimmed with white and red, after a certain well-defined pattern. Then suppose that whole regiments and brigades, and even many great general divisions of that army, should forthwith don a uniform of red, trimmed with orange and green. And imagine that the soldiers wearing this unauthorized uniform should ridicule those who persisted in wearing the exact kind of uniform prescribed by the imperial decree! Would it be too much to say of them that they practically rejected the kingship of the Czar? You say the cases are not parallel, and I confess that they do not exactly coincide, for the Czar, though a great autocrat, is, after all, only a man, and it often happens that he is not even a manly man; but the Lord Jesus is the "King of kings and Lord of lords," and there seems to be no possible pretext for disregarding his decree.

There are, indeed, a few of our pedobaptist friends who dispute about the meaning of his decree respecting baptism, insisting that it does not enjoin an immersion in water. But unfortunately for their claim of loyalty, they all with one accord accept an immersed person as scripturally baptized, thus conceding the very thing insisted upon by Baptists, viz.: that immersion is the baptism enjoined by the decree. But if any are disposed to dissent from this conclusion as unwarranted, and to say that while they accept the immersed as baptized, they still insist that immersion is not the thing commanded, they only make a bad matter worse, for if immersion is not the thing commanded, then to accept it in the place of that thing is to indorse and in the most solemn manner to approve an act of disobedience—to call that obedience which they know is not obedience. If this is loyalty to Christ, it is certainly loyalty of a very strange sort, such as none of the princes of this world will ever be apt to covet toward themselves.

But perhaps you will ask, "Are Baptists

better than pedobaptists? are they more holy, or more loyal to Christ?" And it may be that, like some very good people whom I have met, you will deem these questions quite unanswerable. But wait a little. Has not some one said, To obey is better than sacrifice? If this be true (and it is the word of the Lord by the mouth of the prophet Samuel), does it not follow that of two professed disciples of Christ, in all other respects alike, but differing in this, that one seeks to obey him in all things, while the other is content to obey him in some things only, and in other things live in open disobedience to his laws, the former will have the divine approval more fully than the latter? Is it not true that, other things being equal, he who is the most obedient is morally the best, the most holy, the most loyal to Christ? These questions admit but one answer, and that answer demonstrates that just in proportion as Baptists are more obedient than pedobaptists, they are more loyal to their King, the Lord Christ.

Said a Methodist lady to her husband, a good Baptist deacon: "My dear, the arguments of your pastor seem very conclusive, but they involve one great difficulty that I can not overcome. If they are true, then Baptists must be better and holier than those who practice sprinkling, and, of course, that can not be."

"I declare," replied the deacon, "I never thought of that. It seems to me you are right about it. We Baptists are all poor, miserable sinners at the best. When we would do good evil is present with us, and we are not holy at all—much less, more holy than pedobaptists. There must be some mistake about this matter, and I will go to town and ask our pastor to explain it."

So to town he went, and submitted the matter to his pastor. When his pastor frankly admitted that those who obey Christ are actually more holy than those who do not obey him, he was greatly astonished, but soon concluded that *Obedience*, other things being equal, *is the true measure of holiness*, and, like a sensible man, he went home and told his wife that, after all, a Baptist brother who *obeys* Christ is a better Christian and a better man than a Methodist brother who refuses to obey him. At the risk, therefore, of being charged with the awful opinion that there is a real difference between those who serve God in an obedient life, and those who do not serve him thus, I persist in calling your attention to this practical and vital issue between Baptists and pedobaptists. And

I beg you consider the relation of Baptists to this issue. They did not make it, and they are in no way responsible for it. They have simply obeyed their King as they are in duty bound to do. They could not do less, without incurring the guilt of disobedience and disloyalty. Confronted by the command of Christ, they must obey or rebel. Prompted alike by love and loyalty, they hasten to obey. Now you must admit they could do no less, without subjecting themselves to very grave censure, to say the least. And you must also admit that, had our pedobaptist friends yielded a like obedience to the command of the King, there could have been no issue between themselves and Baptists about it.

The truth is, that our pedobaptist friends are wholly responsible for the existence of this issue. They have created it, by practically ignoring the Kingship of Christ in certain directions. There stands the command of our Lord enjoining the duty of immersion. It is plain and unequivocal—so plain, indeed, that no pedobaptist ever attempts to translate it by *sprinkle*, or *pour*, or *purify*. So unequivocal, that all pedobaptists who translate it at all, render it by *immerse* or *dip*, or by some other word of the same meaning. And yet, despite these well-known facts, and though confronted on every side by unanswerable arguments against their practice, our pedobaptist brethren persist in substituting sprinkling for immersion, and insist that it will do as well.

The issue is created and maintained, not by Baptists, but by the disobedience of pedobaptists to the mandate of the King, the Lord Jesus, and it must continue until that disobedience ceases. It is neither less nor more than an irrepressible conflict, that can be terminated only by the practical and actual submission of the disobedient to the authority of the King.

For if Baptists, wearied with the strife, were content to ignore it, Christ would raise up some other and more faithful people, to maintain the prerogatives of his crown and the authority of his Kingship. For the issue is primarily between Christ on the one side, and all who contemn his authority on the other—Baptists being a party to it only by reason of their loyalty to their King; whence it is evident that it can terminate only when he is universally and cheerfully obeyed by all who call him Lord. Baptists may prove recreant to their trust, and cease to bear witness to the truth, for they are but erring men; but Christ the Lord has girded himself for the conquest, and he will march on victoriously until his Word shall have become the supreme law of his kingdom, in fact, as well as in profession.

But meantime, the issue remains. Baptists "crown him Lord of all;" and if they fail in their obedience, it is the failure that comes from human weakness and infirmity, not from any boasted superiority of plan or of method, devising some other and "easier" way, that will do "just as well" as his way. And pedobaptists "crown him Lord of all," but continue to disobey him deliberately, and of set purpose, justifying their disobedience by the strange plea: "It is a matter of no importance, and our way will do just as well."

Now, my dear brother, will you tell me what we Baptists can do? If we come over to you, we will become partakers of your disobedience, and of its consequent guilt; and, what seems to us still worse, we will dishonor and grieve our Lord and Master by joining you in ignoring his authority as King.

On the other hand, if we do not come over to you, men will say of us, "They are narrow and bigoted;" and thousands of your people will echo and approve that saying. In this matter we are forced to choose between Christ and a host of his professed disciples whom we greatly love. The dilemma is a very painful one; but much as we love our erring brethren, we love our crucified and risen Lord still more, and we feel constrained at all hazards to obey his words, as loyal subjects of Jesus Christ our King.

Now, my brother, if you regard the Kingship of Christ as a vital fact, you can solve the difficulty, so far as you are concerned, by obeying the King in the ordinance of baptism. If you say that would make you a Baptist, I agree with you most heartily; but certainly a worse thing than that might happen to you. I do not say you can come to us with a good conscience; but rather, that by coming to us honestly and heartily, *you will gain a good conscience*, and *that*, like "godliness with contentment," is "great gain." Nor is this statement one whit too bold; neither is it in the least degree egotistic or uncharitable. For, in common with all pedobaptists, you practically concede that we are right, by gladly receiving such of our members as choose to unite with you, as scripturally baptized. For, if they are scripturally baptized, so are we; and therefore the baptism for which we contend is the true Bible baptism, the whole pedobaptist world being the judges. In coming to us, then, you are stepping upon solid ground; ground that the entire Christian world concedes to be scriptural and true. And you are stepping off from very doubtful ground; from ground that, at the best you can say of it, is very shaky, and, for aught you know, altogether unsafe.

For you will not deny that the things in debate are not the peculiar views and usages of the Baptists, but the peculiar doctrines and practices of pedobaptists. The things in dispute are not believer's baptism, nor immersion—these, like ingots of pure gold, are current everywhere—but they are infant baptism and sprinkling, which a large portion of the Christian world rejects utterly as wholly unscriptural, and which are defended by their friends mainly on the score of convenience, or of churchly authority to change at pleasure the ordinances of the Lord's house.

At present you are standing, and with great difficulty, on an unstable, boggy marsh, that trembles and sinks terribly every time you move even one step. Come over to us, by simply giving up that which you do not know to be true, leaving behind you not one solitary conscientious conviction of right or of duty, but only a lot of doubtful and useless observances, and lo! you will stand upon the solid rock of Bible truth. You know I have tried it, and speak from experience. If you say it is a *costly* change, I admit it, for it is hard to separate from tried friends, but the certainty and comfort it brings are altogether beyond price.

The well-known maxim of the celebrated David Crockett, "Be sure you are right, then go ahead," is certainly a safe one in religion. In dealing with interests of such measureless magnitude, a reasonable certainty is the very least that a cautious and prudent person ought to be satisfied with. Why should any one go on beyond into the region of shadows and of doubt? It is not rational or wise to do so; and there is nothing to be gained by it, except unrest of spirit and possible harm to the soul. And this is eminently true in respect to all the peculiar pedobaptist usages. Even if well-founded, they are not in any way necessary to the integrity or the perpetuity of the Church, nor to the fullness and completeness of the individual Christian character. At the very worst, *immersion is as good as sprinkling*, and *believer's baptism is as valid and as efficacious* as *infant baptism*. Then why not omit the doubtful practices, and adhere to those which are clearly scriptural and right, and which undeniably are sufficient to meet all the wants of the soul? Why not be *sure you are right* before you go ahead in the administration of the solemn ordinances of religion in the name of the Lord? But if you resolve to act upon this just and rational principle, you will never sprinkle another person, either adult or infant. In short, acting on this plain, honest maxim, you will tarry with the Baptists until you depart for the upper sanctuary.

Now, my dear brother, I can not return to my old church home among my pedobaptist friends until this matter of the Kingship of Christ can be in some way reconciled to pedobaptist practices. He says to me, "If ye love me, keep my commandments;" and so long as I honestly strive to keep them, one and all, I can say in reply, "Lord, thou knowest that I love thee;" and, if necessary, I could add, "Behold the proof that I love thee, in that I do keep thy commandments." But should I return to my old church home, and resume the practice of sprinkling, what reply could I make? Would he not say to me, "Why call ye me Lord, Lord, and do not the things that I say?" I confess I do not see how I could expect him to do otherwise. And if I were not a minister, it would be equally impossible for me to unite with any pedobaptist church, for he who bids a wrong-doer God-speed in his wrong-doing is a partaker of his evil deeds. He who aids another in his wrong-doing virtually does the wrong himself.

But perhaps you will say: "Why lay so much stress on the Kingship of Christ in this matter of baptism? If we pedobaptists do not perfectly obey him in regard to baptism, neither do Baptists perfectly obey him in other matters. Surely, our Baptist brethren will not claim that they always keep all of his commandments. They know and confess that they do not. Then why make so much ado because we fail on this particular one?"

You voice a difficulty over which many good people stumble—a difficulty which has led many honest seekers after the truth to conclude that Baptists are not sincere in pressing upon others the Kingship of Christ, and that they urge it chiefly to further their own peculiar denominational interests. I well remember a time when I viewed the matter in exactly that light, and I said to our Baptist friends, just as the irreligious often say to earnest Christian workers, "Physician, heal thyself."

But a little reflection will show that the difficulty is only apparent, not real. For the conceded failure of the Baptists to keep perfectly all the commandments of the King arises, not from any disposition to undervalue any of them, as of little or no importance, nor from any attempt to set aside any of them on the plea that something else will do as well as the thing specifically required by our Lord, but only from that "weakness of the flesh" of which Baptists partake in common with others, but of which they certainly have no monopoly.

But the failure of our pedobaptist friends to obey the command to baptize arises from a very different source. Sometimes, indeed, it is due to ignorance of the true meaning of the command, but more generally, as you well know, it springs from an utter indifference to the command, as a thing of no importance, or still worse, from a strong aversion to the thing commanded, as inconvenient, or indelicate, or rude and barbarous. Not infrequently it arises from a selfish, partisan spirit, that dares to put the usage of a sect above the command of Christ. I do not need to quote any one to prove these statements, for no wide-awake man can move about in pedobaptist circles for a single year, in any community in our land, without meeting with many painful evidences of their truth.

It is one thing, through sheer weakness, to

fail here and there to render that full and perfect obedience to every commandment, which is due from every loyal subject of our King, and quite another thing to treat any one or more of his commands with indifference or contempt, and persistently to refuse obedience to it on the plea that it is a thing of no consequence, or that something else will do quite as well as the thing commanded.

But why should Baptists wait until they shall have attained to perfection of obedience, before preaching the duty of obedience to pedobaptists? Are none but the perfect to preach the truth to others? Do pedobaptists wait until they have become sinless before preaching the duty of repentance to other sinners? Do they refrain from rebuking sin in the ungodly because they are themselves not altogether free from faults? But if not, why blame the Baptists for declining to wait until they are faultless before they point out the glaring faults of others? If only the perfect may preach the gospel of righteousness, and press the authority of Christ upon the hearts and consciences of men, who will hold forth the "word of life," or presume to utter one word in favor of good morals, or attempt to define and defend Christian ethics.

There is an eminent fitness in the command

enjoining baptism, to test the loyalty of Christains. It is a positive command, resting not so much on the nature of things, as upon the will of its author. Every moral precept commends itself to each man's judgment and conscience as reasonable and right in itself. We can very easily see that obedience will be attended with many advantages. Every one understands that, in the long run, morality pays, that honesty is the best policy, and that truthfulness, purity, kindliness, generosity and moderation contribute to health, comfort and temporal prosperity. A man, therefore, may cheerfully obey all those precepts, conducing to such desirable results, from purely personal and selfish considerations, without one thought of loyalty to their author. It follows that such precepts afford no certain test of loyalty to Christ, since even the deist and the atheist often conform to them, as the surest way of winning honor and success in the affairs of this life. But not so with baptism. There is no evident, undeniable utility in it. No one would care to observe it for its own sake. Humanly speaking, it is not the best policy. Rantism is much easier, and usually it is far more popular. And it must be conceded that, in itself, it is quite as effective as immersion. Why, then, should any one be immersed?

Can any one assign any other good reason for it than simply that Christ requires it? I confess frankly that this is the only reason that I know of, and it brings each one to a test, and a severe one, of loyalty to Christ.

Aside from the command and the example of our Lord, immersion is inconvenient and sometimes unsightly. At all events, it is not always beautiful in itself, and it adds nothing to manly dignity or womanly grace. And its symbolic meaning is not, by any means, flattering to the self-esteem of the average man. But when we remember that the authority of Christ is back of it, then it challenges obedience, and tests each man's loyalty to our Lord, in a degree altogether unequaled by any other precept of the Holy Scriptures.

Is it not fitting, therefore, that Baptists should urge all men to obey it? And is it strange that they should decline to do anything indorsing the conduct of those who refuse to comply with this plain mandate of the Master? In all this they do only that which, as true subjects of Christ, they are in duty bound to do. Will you end the controversy by obeying our King?

Fraternally yours, ———.

III.

SECTARIANISM A CURSE.

"Mark them which cause divisions [lit., twofold upstandings], and avoid them."—PAUL.

MY DEAR BROTHER:—All true Baptists believe in the unity of the Churches of Christ. Believing in the Holy Scriptures as the Word of God, they can not think otherwise than that our Lord designed that his churches should be one body, as he, its head, is one head. Not, indeed, that they should be one in the sense of a great overshadowing hierarchy, such as the Papacy; nor a vast centralized system of organic oneness such as Presbyterianism, or Lutheranism, or Methodism, with a complicated and cumbrous mass of machinery, ruling assemblies, conferences and bishops, and subordinated churches, or fragments of churches, and a subordinated clergy chained by a set of man-made rules, which they may not amend, but must constantly and carefully obey. All these contrivances, together with all types of episcopacy, are among the "many inventions" which good men, and some not so good, have devised from time to time to steady the ark of God, or to further interests and ambitions not altogether saintly.

I do not know of any Baptist who believes that the Apostolic Churches in Jerusalem and Antioch were, in any *organic* sense, one church. They were two bodies organically, separate and distinct each from the other, each one of them a complete church in itself, without borrowing anything from the other, and each one independent of the other in the sense that it did not derive any part of its authority, its rights or its privileges from the other. And yet they were alike in their organic structure, each being in itself a pure democracy, yet each recognizing the one King and Lawgiver, the Lord Jesus Christ.

And these two Apostolic Churches were one in doctrine, in ordinances, in spirit, in aims and in work. They believed in the same Lord, rejoiced in the same salvation, rested upon the same hope, held forth the same Word of Life, taught the same truths, engaged in the same work—the evangelization of the world—and practiced the self-same baptism—the immersion of the professed believer.

Though organically distinct, there was a real and wonderful unity—a oneness of form, of faith and of practice—that made them true yoke-fellows in the spirit and in the work of the Master. There was no "upstanding" of the one against the other, no clashing of views, of practices or of interests. In organization, authority, rights and duties, they were *two* churches; but in doctrine, spirit, purpose and ordinances, they were *one* church, the one body of Christ.

And this is the sort of unity of the churches in which Baptists devoutly believe, as that which the Master desires, and for which he so earnestly prays, "That they all may be one; as thou, Father, art in me, and I in thee, that they also may be one in us: *that the world may believe that thou hast sent me.*" And this, too, is the divine unity which he will ultimately secure among his people throughout the whole earth, and for which he has not only prayed, but also has made ample provision. Listen to his own wonderful description of the means by which it is to be brought about, and the vast and beneficent results which will surely follow its accomplishment: "And the glory which thou gavest me I have given them; that they may be one, even as we are one: I in them and thou in me, that they may be made perfect in one: and that the world may know that thou hast sent me, and hast loved them as thou hast loved me."

Now ponder these wonderful words. His own glory—the glory that he received of the Father—the Master has given to his people; he has actually committed it to their keeping, and they are entrusted with it to-day, that they may be one. The great end is twofold: first, that they may be one; and then, as a result of this oneness, that the "world may know" two things vital to its welfare—first, "that thou hast sent me," and then that "thou hast loved them as thou hast loved me." What is that glory? Whatever else it may be, it must include his honor as the Christ of God, his reputation and character as the Savior of men, the vindication of his authority as King of saints, and the full restoration of his Word to its rightful place as the supreme law of his entire Church to the end of time. Vastly more than this it doubtless includes, all that communicable grace and Christlikeness which is the fruit of the indwelling of the Comforter in the hearts of his people; but less than this it certainly can not imply.

Here, then, is a mighty trust, which is at once an endowment of power ever growing, and the imposition of a duty ever expanding in its proportions and world-wide in its tremendous scope and its measureless consequences; and its first object is the *unity* of his churches and of his people, *that they may be one*.

It is practically the impartation of the Christ himself to his people, to bring about this grand, godlike unity of his disciples in the coming ages, and therefore that coming unity is already a thing graciously assured. Then, through this unity, will come an overwhelming conviction in the mind and the conscience of the world, that the Church of Christ is really something more than a great company of fanatics, pretenders and enthusiasts; that, in very deed, the living God does love them, and that his power is upon them; and in the light of this wonderful fact, the *world will come to know* that the Father sent the Son on his great mission and labor of love.

And by far the greatest and most potent of all the mistakes of Christian people in this age, as in ages past, is the mistake of the "*twofold upstanding*," or the cultivation of divisions, and the building up of sects and parties among themselves. Jesus prays "that they all may be one; that the world may believe that thou hast sent me;" and the great apostle to the Gentiles writes: "Now I beseech you, brethren, by the name of our Lord Jesus Christ, that ye all speak the same thing, and *that there be no divisions* [margin, *schisms*] *among you;* but that you be perfectly joined together in the *same mind* and in the *same judgment.*" And a little later he writes: "Now I beseech you, brethren, *mark them which cause divisions* [lit., twofold *up-standings, i. e.*, parties or sects] and offenses, contrary to the doctrine which ye have learned, *and avoid them.*" And again still later he writes: "I, therefore, the prisoner of the Lord, beseech you that ye walk worthy of the vocation wherewith ye are called, with all lowliness and meekness, with long-suffering, forbearing one another in love; endeavoring to keep the unity of the Spirit in the bond of peace. There is one body [evidently meaning the Church, which he elsewhere calls the body of Christ], and one Spirit, even as ye are called in one hope of your calling; one Lord, one faith, one baptism, one God and Father of all, who is above all, and through all, and in you all." And the same great apostle enumerates as a part of the "works of the flesh," "factions, divisions, heresies" (margin, *parties*), and says: "That they which practice such things shall not inherit the kingdom of God."

Now I am sure that these words of our Lord, and of his apostle, do not mean *cultivate* "a vigorous denominationalism." No man can, by any ingenuity, torture them into the support of any such ism. Whitewash things as you will, yet the fact remains that a denomination is neither less nor more than a sect, and a sect is one of the "works of the flesh," not one of the "fruits of the Spirit," Paul himself, taught by the Holy Spirit, being judge. And if those who are the getters-up of a sect "shall not inherit the kingdom of God," as inspiration declares, those who cherish existing sects, and who so constantly counsel the cultivation of a "vigorous denominationalism," can hardly be acting under the guidance of the Spirit of God. Wise men and very great "doctors" they may be, but in this matter they are strangely opposed to Christ and to his Holy Word.

But you will ask: "Are not the Baptists a sect?" I reply, first: If they are a sect, they are not of God; and, second: So far as they may have imbibed the spirit of a sect, they are not approved of God; and, third: That they are not a sect at all, but true gospel churches. The broad line of demarkation between a sect and the "churches of Christ" is this: That the former has some peculiar characteristics of doctrine or of practice which it cherishes for its own sake, and which it will not submit to the test of the Divine Word, rigorously applied, while the latter hold every one of their doctrines, and each one of their practices, at all times, subject to correction by that Word. The one seeks chiefly the honor of the Master by a strict conformity to his revealed will; the other, the honor and growth of a party, by fidelity to its usages and traditions. Tested by these criteria the Baptist churches are not a sect, for with them the Word of God is at all times paramount. They willingly subject all their doctrines and usages to that supreme rule, and they are ever ready to renounce any doctrine, or custom, or practice, that may be condemned by it. Absolute conformity to the law of Christ in all things is their controlling desire. Not what is most convenient, or most popular, nor what their fathers did, but what the Lord Jesus requires, is the rule of their faith and of their practice. That they are alone in this, may seem to you a very bold and reckless statement, but, before you denounce it too severely, be so kind as to name some pedobaptist denomination that holds the same attitude of entire subjection to the authority of Christ.

Surely, those who openly and boldly claim that some way other than that which Christ commands will do equally well, or that anything that he has commanded is a matter of no importance, and may be innocently ignored or changed at pleasure, either do not accept the Word of Christ as the final word in their hearts, or they fail amazingly in obeying it in their lives.

As a Baptist, therefore, I have a right to arraign the current sectarianism as the chief hindrance to that unity of Christ's people, which must precede the ingathering of the nations into his fold.

Some years ago, while pastor in the city of M——, I received a call from a very intelligent lady, a member of the Catholic Church in that place, who came to consult me about her spiritual interests. The Lord had already "opened her eyes to behold wondrous things out of his law"—and she was secretly, and yet tremblingly, hoping in Christ. "Being justified by faith," she was "a disciple of Jesus, but secretly, for fear of" the Romanists. In one of our interviews I asked her why it is that so few of our Roman Catholic neighbors come to a knowledge of the truth as it is in Jesus. Said I: "Why is it that they do not read the Bible for themselves?" And this is substantially, and almost verbatim, her reply: "Many of them do begin to read the Bible, anxious to learn the truth, but their Catholic friends laugh at them. 'Look at the Protestant world,' say they; 'do they not all take that Bible for their guide? And yet they are divided into a great number of sects, no two of which can agree about the meaning of that book. Can a book so hard to be understood be a revelation from God? And if its own best friends can not understand it alike, how can you hope to arrive at any definite knowledge of its true meaning? You are not wiser than all the rest of mankind, but you ought to be wise enough to let that old book alone, and believe firmly in the Holy Mother Church.' And in most cases," continued my informant, "the anxious, inquiring Catholic is persuaded to give up the study of the Bible, the sectarian divisions of the Protestants seeming to him a convincing proof that it can not be understood by any one, nor render any real service to those who earnestly desire to know the truth."

That my informant told the truth, I can not doubt; and accepting her statements as an honest, unvarnished description of the situation, who can fail to see that Protestant sectarianism is one of the strongest bulwarks of Romanism in every Protestant land. It is easy to say that it ought not to be so; that earnest Romanists ought not to be influenced by such considerations to give up the study of God's Word; but that does not change the fact. They are usually in doubt whether, in very truth, it is God's Word, and the multiplicity of Protestant sects very naturally confirms that doubt, and leads them to abandon the examination of a book, apparently so difficult to be understood.

In much the same way multitudes of the world's people are led to neglect the Bible, by the endless divisions and the hopeless wrangles of its professed friends. Indeed, it is a fact, patent to all thoughtful observers, that the sectarian divisions and struggles of the professedly Christian world furnish to infidelity its most plausible excuses—nay, its most terrible and deadly weapons, impeaching at once the inspiration of the Bible and the saving power of the Gospel of Christ.

Nor does the evil stop here. Sectarian dissensions impair the spirituality of the churches until, like Sampson shorn of his locks, they are almost powerless. At the same time they cause an unwise expenditure in the prosecution of the Lord's work, crowding thousands of small towns and villages with an excessive number of weak churches and half-starved ministers, resulting in a fearful struggle for a mere existence that too often degenerates into a bitter rivalry, each with the other, and all of them with those who cater to the appetites and amusement of the public in the hope of gain. In the fierce conflict for an existence, churches whose sole aim should be the salvation of men, convert their places of worship into theaters, cook-shops and gambling dens, where the youth are initiated into the mysteries of religious raffling and pious grab-bags. There, too, they are taught to stake money on bits of ring-cake, or to sell smiles and kisses, for the benefit of the church.

This is no fancy sketch, but a mild picture of scenes actually occurring in this year of grace in hundreds of American communities.

Good men of various sects may say, and many of them do say: "I care nothing for any sect; all churches are equally dear to me." Just now it is fashionable, in many quarters, for pious men to talk in that way. I have heard very many ministers talk in that way, but I have yet to meet the first one whose conduct agrees with such professions. In fact, a somewhat extended and painful experience has taught me to look out sharply for the ministers who are so liberal—in words. They generally prove themselves shepherds who are in search of more sheep; and if they chance to look for them in your fold, you need not be greatly surprised.

If these things be true—and no man can disprove them—the only way to eradicate sectarianism is to destroy the sects whence it necessarily flows. Sectism must go, or sectarianism will assuredly stay, and continue indefinitely its deadly work.

How can sectism be banished from the Christian world? Not by force. That is always a failure. It has been tried a thousand years, and applied in a thousand ways, and all in vain. Men can not be coërced by fagot and sword into thinking alike. Persecution fortifies and multiplies sects. The more force, the less unity, is one of the great lessons of the past. Beside all that, it is an unscriptural and an unholy method, a daring usurpation of that authority which belongs to God alone, an act of tyranny which it is the duty of all men of every creed to resist to the utmost. No man, be he Pope or cardinal, bishop or priest, king or conqueror, has any right whatever to "lord it over God's heritage," or to even attempt to compel the consciences of men to assent to any dogma whatever, no matter how true or how important that dogma may be. Christ alone is king in the domain of conscience, and to him alone, is each human soul answerable for its want of faith, or its wrong faith, and its opinions, whether right or wrong.

And the growing recognition of this fact encourages us to hope that the days of "bloody persecution" have passed away, never to return, at least in this favored land; and that the sun of religious liberty has at last arisen, nevermore to suffer eclipse, or to sink beneath the horizon.

But if sectism can not be put away by force, neither can it be cajoled into inaction by compromises. This generation has witnessed repeated attempts in this direction. Men of good repute, of honest intent and vigorous thought, have cried out: "Away with creeds, and let us unite, no matter how diverse our doctrinal views, on this broad platform: Christian character the only test of church membership;" and thousands have heeded the cry, and constituted churches on that basis. But those creedless churches have become at once a sect of the most stringent sort, with a creed all the more defective and unyielding because unwritten, and with a membership so heterogeneous that they can do little more than admire the "liberal," but impracticable platform on which their churches are constructed.

And, in the nature of things, every such attempt to attain unity by sacrificing or ignoring truth, is a predestined failure. In its largest possible success, it merely brings together into one body all the divergent views and irreconcilable differences of the various sects, by which it is at once stricken as by an incurable moral paralysis. And it is well that it is so, for the unity that can be attained only by ignoring divine truth is always the unity of moral death. Better a vigorous sectism, fighting over dogmas supposed to embody important revealed truth, than the unity of total indifference to principles. A church that is in a constant dread of itself, that forever alternates between volcanic eruptions and Arctic silence and death, is of little use to itself or to any one else, except to illustrate the folly and futility of seeking Christian unity by the sacrifice of Christian principles.

Now, my dear brother, since neither force nor compromises can put away sectism and secure that unity of Christ's people for which he so earnestly prays, there remains but one other method by which to seek a consummation so devoutly to be desired, and that is by inculcating an honest and strict observance of the "Law of Christ" in all things—in doctrines, in ordinances and in the organization of churches.

And this is, if you please, the Baptist plan—that is, the plan that they adhere to; the old gospel plan that was successful in the primitive churches. Baptists did not invent it; they do not claim any peculiar right to it; but they have great confidence in it, and they have long proved their fidelity to it. They firmly believe there is no other way to attain to Christian unity and its blessed fruits but to make the Word of God, honestly and faithfully interpreted, the supreme rule of Christian faith and practice. That it is likely to prove a slow way, they concede; but though slow, it is sure, and sooner or later it must prove a success.

And in this confidence, they remain firm in their loyalty to the Word of Christ, seeking thereby the overthrow of that sectarianism that is so hateful to all who deeply sympathize with our Lord in his desire that his people may be one, and so hurtful to souls and to all the interests of the churches of Christ.

So, my dear brother, if I do not accept your

kind invitation to return to my old church home, I trust you will do me the justice to attribute my conduct to those causes that dictate it. I desire the union of all Christians as earnestly as any one; but I can not seek it by means that my judgment and conscience utterly condemn, and that I could not hope to justify to the Master.

But you can come to the one gospel standard of doctrine and of duty as I came, and together we can labor hopefully for the unity of the Church. Yours, ———.

IV.
TESTIMONY OF THE LEXICONS.

"In the multitude of counselors there is safety."
—SOLOMON.

MY DEAR BROTHER:—Since the issue between Baptists and pedobaptists involves great questions of Bible fact, it calls for a careful and thorough study of the language of that blessed book touching the matters which are so sharply controverted. Of course, such an exhaustive investigation of questions so broad and so many-sided is quite impossible within the limits of these friendly and informal letters. Nor is it necessary that we attempt a work so great, as if it were a task hitherto wholly neglected. It is a work on which multitudes—men of genius, learning and piety—have wrought with wonderful patience, ability and success in the ages past, and we have entered into their labors. They have accumulated vast stores of facts bearing directly or remotely on the general theme; facts well-authenticated, which we may safely and wisely accept as indisputable, and which we may use with confidence in making up our judgment. Many of these facts have been established by men laboring in the interests, not of any sect, or party, or religious usage, or custom, but of sound learning and a pure literature. These are the more trustworthy, because the results of an impartial study, and so evidently correct that they have long commanded the full and unanimous assent of investigators and educators of every sect in Christendom.

Of course, it is not needful that any preliminary work, which has already been done so thoroughly and so ably, be done over again by us. The student of mathematics is not obliged by slow and laborious processes to verify the multiplication table. It is enough that he should learn the table, and acquire the necessary skill to use it properly. Even so in our Bible study those things that are thoroughly known, and universally accepted as unquestionably true by every one competent to judge, we may justly use as data on which to base our conclusions in those matters of greater importance to which they stand related. And especially is this true in respect to that large class of facts, which, each and all, have been verified from age to age in the most thorough manner by competent scholars.

Acting in harmony with these plain and undeniable facts, I intend not to inflict upon you any prosy, interminable discussion of facts already thoroughly established, but merely to call your attention to a series of such facts, and the witnesses by whom they are attested, in a way that makes any further debate about them altogether unnecessary, if not presumptuous. These facts are the raw material, if you please, out of which it is not difficult to construct the only true and tenable interpretation of the Scriptures on the subjects to which they relate. And first among these facts, both in the order of nature, and in its bearing on the issue before us, permit me to name this one—

THE TESTIMONY OF THE LEXICONS.

You are well aware, my dear brother, that *baptizo* and its derivatives, which are used by our Lord and his apostles to indicate baptism, are Greek words. In that language, as you are also well aware, they have a well-defined meaning, and that meaning is their true sense in the Holy Scriptures. In the old English Bible they were translated by the word *dip* and its derivatives. The readers of that Bible could not be in doubt respecting the *act* of baptism. As they read of "John the *dipper*," they could not fail to understand his words, "I, indeed, *dip* you in water," nor could they fail to understand how Jesus "was *dipped* of John into the Jordan." And as they read, "Go ye, therefore, and teach all nations, *dipping* them," etc., or those other words, "He that believeth and is *dipped* shall be saved," they could not have any rational doubt that the scriptural baptism is an immersion. But when that old Bible gave place to the authorized version of King James, there came a change. The Greek words for baptism were not translated, but simply transferred. And as sprinkling had already come into use in France, and in some other continental countries, and was daily growing in popularity among the English nobility as the favorite method of fashionable christening, the transferred words soon came to be used in a new and peculiar sense. For the christening, after it had ceased to be a *dipping*, was still called a *baptism*. In this way, by a gradual, but sure process, was coined the new *English* word, *baptize*, with a meaning altogether foreign to that of the old Greek word, being used to designate the *rite* of baptism without any reference to the *method* of it. Thus it became, and thus it remains to this day, a merely technical name for a religious ordinance, which, as a matter of fact, has long been administered in multitudes of Protestant churches, in various ways, as fashion, taste, or mere caprice may demand.

And this technical sense of this English word *baptize* is unconsciously or ignorantly attributed by the average reader to the *transferred*, anglicized Greek word in the Scriptures, leading him to infer, most erroneously, that baptism is a religious ceremony, to be observed in any way to please the taste. And it is a fact not creditable to our English Protestantism, that this palpable mistake is generally winked at, and often actively confirmed by men who, to speak with the utmost charity, *ought* to know better. Yet this deception, transparent and unwarrantable as it is, constitutes one of the chief defenses of the practice of sprinkling.

Now, my brother, it must be evident to you, and to every thoughtful person, that this technical English word, *baptize*, which is not yet three hundred years old, ought not to be permitted to determine the meaning of the old Greek word used by our Lord and his apostles. That word they must have used, not in the sense of this modern English form of it, but in its old, legitimate Greek sense; in that sense in which it was then used and understood by their auditors, and by those who wrote and spoke the Greek language. For it is a rule in all languages, and of universal application in all ages and among all classes of men, that THE WORDS OF A WRITER OR SPEAKER ARE TO BE TAKEN IN THE SENSE CURRENT AT THE TIME WHEN THEY WERE USED, AND AMONG THE PEOPLE TO WHOM THEY WERE ADDRESSED. This rule is so obviously just that it needs no defense, and so plain that it requires no explanation. And it is equally indispensable in every department of human thought and investigation. The jurist applies it in determining the meaning of the constitution and the laws; the historian applies it in deciding the facts of history; the scientist rests upon it in exploring the scientific lore of the ages past; the linguist relies upon it in the study of the languages; the court depends upon it in construing the wills of the dead, and the contracts, agreements and obligations of the living. And unless we regard it in the study of the Bible, we might as well close the sacred volume at once, for its just interpretation will be forever impossible. For, although it is the Word of God, it is given to us in the language of men, in the terms and subject to the laws of human language, and only by means of a just application of those laws can we know definitely its true meaning. Many good people ignore this plain truth in their treatment of the Scriptures, telling us that the Word of God is spiritual, that we are to seek its inner, spiritual sense, and that only not, by the application of any rules of interpretation, good or bad, but by prayer and a reverent contemplation.

It is very true that the Bible treats of spiritual things, and that a reverent, prayerful spirit is indispensable to a right study of it; but it is also true that it treats of those spiritual verities and duties in the terms of human speech, and in accordance with the recognized laws of such speech. And only as we apply those laws in its interpretation, by means of a sanctified common sense, can we unlock the treasures stored in its pages, and attain with certainty the Truth of God, rather than the dreams of a pious but imperfect heart, led astray by the creations of a devout but erring imagination.

If we would know what baptism really is, what is the action that constitutes it, we must seek such knowledge by the careful study of the words of our Lord in commanding it as they were understood in that age, and by the people of whose language they were a familiar, well-known part. The question is not, What does the word *baptize* mean in London, or in New York, in the year 1885? but What did it mean among the Greeks in Athens, in Alexandria, in Jerusalem, in the days of our Lord and of his apostles? For its ancient Greek meaning is, undeniably, its true sense in the Holy Scriptures.

How, then, shall we ascertain that meaning? When we desire to learn the true sense of an English word, we do not usually attempt to trace its use throughout the entire body of English literature. Life is too short, and time too precious for that, but we turn to an English dictionary or lexicon, and in a moment we are satisfied. In our standard English dictionaries we recognize a full and competent authority on the sense of English words. They are carefully compiled by competent scholars, who have made the study of our language the work of their lives, giving us the benefit of their laborious investigations in a compact and convenient form. We place them in our homes and in our schools, depending upon them ourselves, and encouraging our children to consult them as authoritative exponents of our mother tongue.

We have also dictionaries or lexicons of the Greek language, giving the meaning of Greek words in plain English. They have been prepared by eminent Greek scholars, with great care and immense labor. They have the indorsement of the learned world, and they are in constant use in our higher institutions of learning.

Take the Greek-English Lexicon of Liddell and Scott. Its compilers belong to the Church of England, but its admirers and indorsers belong to all churches, including men of all creeds and men of no creed. In all the colleges of all denominations in England and in America it is deservedly held in the highest estimation.

Of this great work a new edition (the seventh) has lately been issued, and in it we have the following:

BAPTIZO—*To dip in or under water; to sink, to bathe, to baptize.*

BAPTISMOS—*A dipping in water—baptism.*

BAPTISMA—*Baptism.*

BAPTISTES—*One that dips—a baptizer.*

And with these definitions there is a substantial agreement among all lexicographers. Sophocles, Donnegan, Rost and Palm, Parkhurst, Stephanus, Robinson, Wright, Schleusner, Dunbar, Leigh, Schrevelius, Scapula, Bass, Suidas, Morel, Laing, Hederic, Greenfield, Ewing, Jones, Schœttgen, T. S. Green, Suicer, Mintert, Pasor, Grove, Bretschneider, Stokius, Robertson, Passow, Schwarzius, Alstedius, Pickering, Rouma, Gazes, Bagster and Sons, Anthon, Grimm and Cremer—all these say substantially the same thing, defining *baptizo* by *dip*, *plunge*, *immerse* or *submerge*. In the language of Moses Stuart, we may justly say: "All critics and lexicographers of any note are agreed in this." Here, then, are more than forty thoroughly competent witnesses; men who voice the judgment, and enjoy the hearty indorsement of the entire learned world; men who can not be accused of any partiality for the views of Baptists; men whose testimony is embodied in great standard works—at least three of them—Grimm, Cremer and Bagster, on New Testament Greek, and they all, with one accord, assure us that *baptizo* means to *dip*, to *immerse*. Now what shall we do with this great mass of evidence? If we reject it, the scholarship of the world will laugh at us, and deem us ignorant and very conceited; but if we accept it, then we must admit that, after all, "the Baptists are right." Doubtless this sounds very strange to you, for you have probably long been accustomed to think of the Baptists as an ignorant set, having little more than a superstitious regard for mere forms, to justify their tenacious adherence to their peculiar doctrines and usages. But, though it may seem strange, it is yet true, that the scholarship of the Christian world indorses the correctness of the Baptist views of baptism. The truth is, the ignorance and superstition in this matter are *on the other side*. Our pedobaptist friends are, in these things, *walking in darkness*, and fighting the light. They are practically opposing the highest scholarship of Christendom, as well as the explicit command of our Lord, and all this for the sake of usages having their origin in the rankest superstition, and in times of great ignorance.

Now, when you remember that the words *baptize, baptizing, baptized* and *baptism* are not translations of the Greek words, but those words themselves transferred, and changed in their terminal letters, and that their meaning in the Greek of the New Testament is *to dip, to immerse, to bathe*, as all the lexicons tell us, the conclusion is inevitable that *our Lord commands immersion*.

And since he uses always a Greek word that means *to immerse*, one would naturally expect to find it translated by *immerse*. No man has ever yet dared to translate it *to pour*, *to sprinkle* or *to purify*. No set of men dare to print our Lord's command (Matt. xxviii. 19): "Go ye therefore, and teach all nations, *sprinkling* them, or *pouring* them or *purifying* them." Every pedobaptist scholar in the world would protest against that as both wrong and absurd. But how much better is it to transfer the Greek word, instead of translating it, and then pretend that no one can tell what it means, and, under cover of that thin, false pretense, go on sprinkling in the name of Christ. Is this the candor and fair dealing which the world has a right to expect from those who claim reverence and respect as the disciples of the sinless One? Is this double-dealing in sacred things the best way to commend Christianity to honorable men? I would not be too severe upon the translators of our common version. They were in a trying situation. The mandate of a drunken king, who knew how to enforce his decrees by cruel and swift punishments, in a manner compelled them to make the transfer. And back of that royal mandate was the demand of a proud, arrogant nobility for a convenient, tasty christening—one that would admit of a full display of the rich robes of their noble babes. The pressure upon those reverend men was tremendous, and their address to the king, still printed in English editions of their version, shows that they were not the sort of men to endure martyrdom for the truth.

But why should this age perpetuate the great wrong which they were, in a manner, compelled to originate? Why not translate the word honestly and faithfully? Its meaning is plain and definite, quite as plain and definite as that of any other word in the entire Greek Testament, and there is absolutely no room for an intelligent, reasonable doubt about it among thorough biblical scholars. Why, then, is it not translated? Only one true reason can be assigned, and that is, that any possible translation would be fatal to sprinkling.

Let one illustration of this fact suffice: A few years since I asked the Rev. Dr. M.——, an eminent pedobaptist scholar, why it was that he resigned his place on the Committee of Translation of the American Bible Union.

He replied: "When I saw that the committee were determined to translate *baptizo* I resigned, because I did not deem it expedient to translate that word, though, if it must be translated, *immerse* is the proper word by which to render it."

We hear much about the wickedness of the

Papacy in withholding the Word of God from the people, and it is a very grievous wrong; but what shall be said of those Protestants who, by a defective translation, purposely obscure the Word of God, that they may perpetuate the practice of a mere invention of men in his name, in direct contravention of his will? I would not be uncharitable, but if it be not an unpardonable offense, I would suggest that it will be time enough to condemn Rome, when her accusers have given up the practice of unscriptural Romish innovations and have given to the people an honest and complete translation of the Divine Word. The compliant weakness of King James' translators, resulting as it did in a mutilated Bible, has robbed English-speaking people of a clear statement of an important part of the law of Christ for nearly three hundred years.

And this fearful robbery has been recently perpetuated in the Canterbury Revision, otherwise so valuable, against evident light and knowledge, through bondage to *usage*, and to sectarian interests. Why did not the Canterbury revisers translate *baptizo?* Is it possible they could not discover its meaning? All intelligent people know better than that. Besides, the American Committee have put on record evidence that they do know the meaning of the word. For they desired that it should be rendered *bathe* in Mark vii. 4, and in Luke xi. 38. But if it means *bathe*, in the sense of to immerse, in those places, as undeniably it does, then beyond any doubt it means the same in Matt. xxviii. 19, and in Mark xvi. 16.

Why, then, is it silently transferred in those places where it relates directly to the ordinance of baptism? Why is this obscurity deliberately, wantonly perpetuated in the Canterbury Revision? Only one answer is possible, and that is, that sprinkling may still be perpetuated under the plea of indefiniteness in the command.

My brother, what will you do with the lexicons? I can not return to you until they are disposed of. Are they incorrect? But why, then, are they accepted and honored in all pedobaptist institutions of learning? Why are they put into the hands of students by learned professors of the Greek language and literature, as faithful exponents of the true meaning of Greek words?

And if they are to be trusted in translating the Greek of Homer, why not in translating the Greek of the New Testament? I am sure you will admit there is but one honest, honorable answer. They are correct and authoritative, and just as much so in translating the Scriptures as in translating the "Iliad" or the "Odyssey" or the "Orations of Demosthenes." If I were to say, "The lexicons are false, and therefore I will resume sprinkling," the entire learned world, pedobaptist scholars included, would laugh at me, and say many uncomplimentary things of me. To be honest about it, you know, and so do all scholars, that the lexicons are right about this matter.

Here, then, is the dilemma into which the lexicons put us. If we accept their testimony as true, we must confess that Christ has actually and explicitly made immersion an imperative Christian duty; that his command to baptize is a definite, plain command to *immerse*, and that immersion only is baptism; but if we reject their testimony, we will merit and receive the condemnation of the entire learned world.

This dilemma shuts me up where I am—compels me to remain a Baptist. I am not exactly a coward, but I am not equal to an onslaught upon these strong citadels. And I am afraid that an army of the most learned men in the world, in an attack upon the lexicons, would suffer an inglorious defeat. If it were only a Pope, or a Council, or a comet, one might hope for an ultimate victory. The world would march away and forget the two former bodies while the latter would fly off into the abysses of space, and perhaps forget the world. But these lexicons, here they are and they are here to stay, and all the world, confederate for their overthrow, can not effect it in twice ten thousand years. Their impregnable defense is *their truthfulness.*

It seems a little curious, but the same dilemma that compels me to stay where I am, ought to compel you to come and keep me company; and yet you do not come. Perhaps it has not yet got hold of you; but unless you do some artful dodging, it will catch you presently.

Some evade its grip for a time by an ingenious device. They say: "Oh, well; it may be very true that *baptizo* commonly means to immerse, but then it may not mean just that always. Perhaps it may sometimes mean something else, and if so, perhaps it means something else *in the Scriptures.*" And so they manage to hang on to that *perhaps,* but they find it a very uncomfortable situation, and they are all the time in danger of being sadly humiliated by some crushing *mishap.*

This device, though *ingenious,* is not very

ingenuous, and to those who love the truth it is very *unsafe*. For if it were even true that *baptizo* does sometimes mean something other than to dip or immerse, we would have no right to understand it in that unusual and exceptional sense in the New Testament Scriptures, *unless we could prove that its usual sense is there impossible*. For it is a fundamental rule in the interpretation of any writing or speech, that THE WORDS EMPLOYED IN SUCH WRITING OR SPEECH ARE TO BE UNDERSTOOD IN THEIR USUAL SENSE, UNLESS SOMETHING IN THE SUBJECT ITSELF, OR IN THE CONTEXT, IMPERATIVELY REQUIRES THAT THEY BE TAKEN IN SOME OTHER SENSE.

This rule is too evidently true and just, to need a word of defense. It is undeniably correct, and of universal application. Now suppose for one moment that *baptizo* means to immerse only *seven times in each ten*, that the other three times in each ten it means to sprinkle. Then by our rule, just cited, we must understand it to mean *immerse* in every case where it is not evident that it *can not* mean that; and we could understand it to mean *sprinkle* only in such cases as that the sense *to immerse* would be *evidently forced and untrue*.

In our dispute with Universalists we all use this rule freely, holding them to the *usual* sense of *aiōnios*—everlasting, eternal,—and we are fully warranted in so doing. Indeed, the rule we are considering requires us to do so, as the only means of determining the true sense of the passage.

But if the rule be operative against the Universalist, why is it not operative against the pedobaptist? Surely, you ought yourself to observe a rule of interpretation which you rigidly enforce against others. But the moment you consent to do that, you establish immersion as the scriptural act of baptism, beyond any decent peradventure. That great American statesman, Henry Clay, said: "I would rather be right than be President." Is it too much to expect you to say, "I would rather be right than be a pedobaptist"? If that be your noble purpose, I shall anticipate your speedy arrival in the Baptist camp. At all events, a similar purpose landed me here, and persistently keeps me here. If I am tempted to arise and return to the pedobaptist fold, I am instantly confronted by the great army of Greek lexicographers, telling me, with one voice, that *immersion alone is baptism;* and in the face of this great array of witnesses, I dare not substitute sprinkling for the baptism Christ commands us to perform. Dare you?

Fraternally yours,

V.

CONCESSIONS OF PEDOBAPTIST WRITERS.

"Why call ye me Lord, Lord, and do not the things which I say?"—JESUS.

MY DEAR BROTHER:—If you find some parts of this letter rather dull reading, please do not skip them, for they are the words of good, solid, old pedobaptist saints. It is true, they are giving rather unpalatable evidence, and they do it reluctantly; but you know that testimony extorted from an unwilling witness, by the force of truth alone, is always valuable. And if it tends to establish some fact or proposition in any degree inimical to the known wishes, feelings, practices or interests of the witness, that fact greatly enhances its value. And of this nature are the concessions of many eminent pedobaptist divines, scholars and historians concerning baptism. They are contrary to the general views and practices of the writers and of their churches. No one can account for them except on the ground of a moral necessity—that they are required by the facts, and that their authors, being conscientious, truthful men, could not say less. And this fact assures us also that these reluctant concessions are not overdrawn. We may safely conclude that each one of these interested and intelligent witnesses, testifying against himself, will say no more than the truth fairly obliges him to say. The danger lies in a direction exactly opposite—that he will say far less than he ought to say, since even good men are not prone to tread too heavily on their own precious corns. If they must condemn their own opinions or practices in any respect, even saints will usually do it as gently and as sparingly as possible, having a tender and wholesome regard for their own feelings.

Here are two men, both good men, both pious and truthful, one a Baptist and the other a Presbyterian, and we summon them as witnesses respecting baptism. We ask the first one whether the Greek for *baptism* means *to immerse*, and he says it does. But instinctively we discount his testimony somewhat, thinking more or less definitely: "He is a Baptist, and perhaps he is swayed in some degree by prejudice or self-interest or pride of opinion or denominational feeling. He is an interested witness, and his testimony favors his own side. It may be that his desire to have it so influences his judgment unduly, so that he is not a safe judge in the matter, and we must weigh his evidence with great caution." Then we turn to the second man, propose the same question, and receive the same answer. But we are naturally—well, inevitably—far more impressed by it. We say: "This man is a Presbyterian. We know from his practice of sprinkling that he does not desire to promote immersion. All his prejudices, interests and denominational feelings are opposed to it. Yet he has deliberately given us an answer that condemns his own practice and vindicates that of the Baptist. Why has he done this? It must be for the simple reason that, as an honest man, he could not do otherwise. He agrees with the Baptist, not because he wants to, but because the truth compels him to do so, even against all his own interests, prejudices and preferences." And we are compelled to accept his testimony, and allow it great weight. And it is evidently of great value to every one who desires to know the truth, for it is given, not under any constraint, but freely; not from self-interest, but against it; not at the dictation of party spirit, but against it; not at the behest of prejudice, but against it; not to inflate denominational pride, but inevitably to humiliate it.

Now, my brother, it will not do to say that the continued practice of sprinkling by this Presbyterian witness neutralizes his testimony against it, for that is manifestly untrue. The practice is continued on other grounds—usually on the plea that it is "a matter of indifference," that sprinkling "will do as well," and a great many other similar pleas.

But the testimony which a man gives condemning his own practice is one thing, and the plea by which he may seek to justify that practice in spite of that adverse testimony is quite another thing; and each one must be judged on its own merits. The testimony which an intelligent man gives against himself is very certain to be found true, while the plea by which he seeks to excuse himself for continuing to do the thing condemned, is very apt to prove a mere make-shift, to avoid a disagreeable change of practice and of ecclesiastical relations.

If I admit that Christ commands me to immerse, I am bound to immerse; but if I nevertheless continue to sprinkle, and seek to justify myself by the plea that it is a matter of indifference, or that sprinkling will do just as well, my plea assumes the truth of my admission. Whether the plea is a valid one, is quite another matter. Of that every man must judge for himself. It assumes either that obedience to the known command of Christ is a matter of indifference, or that men are competent to revise and improve his mandates, and are at liberty to do so at their own pleasure. Such assumptions are very daring at the best, and those that act upon them are very bold. Those who are tempted to do so will do well to remember that to "obey is better than sacrifice."

For my own part, while I am not "righteous overmuch," I deem it more pleasant and agreeable, as well as wiser and safer, to obey the Master. He knows what is best for us in this matter, as in everything else, and his great love for us, coupled with his matchless wisdom, fairly challenges compliance with his slightest wish. But when we remember that this dear friend is also our Divine King, and that he has embodied his wish in a positive command, it seems almost incredible that any one, calling himself a citizen of his kingdom, should for one moment presume to disregard his known will. But if any choose to do a thing so daring and unnatural, they must take all the risk of it, nor wonder if to me and to many more the humbler and narrower path of obedience seems the more inviting, the wiser and the safer. For those who think differently, and whose testimony on this subject condemns their practice, I have no word of reproach. I am not their judge. To their own Master they must stand or fall. Their example I view as a dangerous mistake; but their testimony against their own practices I gratefully accept as a valuable, though reluctant, tribute to the truth. Such witnesses are very numerous, and their numbers are constantly and rapidly increasing. In these letters I place before you many decisive testimonies from different writers, all of them men of conceded ability, men eminent for learning, men of reputed piety, and each one of them undeniably a thoroughly competent witness against his own practice and against the practice of his Church.

Among them are leading church historians, great reformers, eminent expositors, noted bishops, eloquent preachers, profound theologians, and famous scholars and writers. They are representative men, belonging to nearly every pedobaptist sect of any prominence in

Christendom. In the list are Catholics and Lutherans, Episcopalians and Presbyterians, Reformed and Remonstrants, Methodists and Congregationalists. They are of many nationalities, English and German, Scotch and Swiss, French, Italian and American.

And this great variety of position and work, of denominational relation and preference, and of nativity and language, is a matter of much importance, lifting their testimonies above the suspicion of any taint of local influence.

Yet, despite all their diversities of creed and of tongue, their testimony to the truth is characterized by a beautiful and convincing unity that can hardly fail to impress you as conclusive. Take first some of the

TESTIMONIES OF EMINENT PEDOBAPTIST HISTORIANS.

MOSHEIM—*Church History, First Century.*—"The sacrament of baptism was administered in this century, without the public assemblies, in places appointed and prepared for that purpose, and was performed by an *immersion of the whole body* in the baptismal font." Of baptism in the *second* century he says: "The persons that were to be baptized, after they had repeated the creed, confessed and renounced their sins, and particularly the devil and his pompous allurements, *were immersed under water*, and received into Christ's kingdom."

I quote from McLaine's translation, Vol. I., pages 126 and 206. Mosheim was an eminent Lutheran scholar and divine, Chancellor and Professor of Theology in the University of Gottingen. His translator, Dr. McLaine, was an eminent pedobaptist clergyman.

NEANDER—*Church Hist.*—"In respect to the form of baptism, it was, *in conformity with the original institution* and the original import of the symbol, *performed by immersion*, as a sign of entire baptism into the Holy Spirit, of being entirely penetrated by the same." In his *History of the Planting and Training of the Church*, the same writer says: "Baptism was originally administered by immersion, and many of the comparisons of Paul allude to this form of administration."

In an appendix to *Judd's Review of Stuart* is a note from Neander, in which he says:

"As to your question on the original rite of baptism, there can be no doubt whatever that, in the primitive times, the ceremony was performed by *immersion*, to signify a *complete immersion* into the new principle of life divine, which was to be imparted by the Messiah. When Paul says that through baptism we are buried with Christ, and rise again with him, he *unquestionably* alludes to the symbol of *dipping into*, and *rising again out of*, the water. The *practice of immersion in the first century was, beyond all doubt, prevalent in the whole Church.*"

Neander has probably no superior as a Christian scholar and historian. The single fact that he was a Professor of Theology in the University of Berlin *thirty-eight years* attests his learning and his competency as a witness.

AUGUSTI—*Archæology.*—"Immersion in water was general until the *thirteenth century* among the Latins. It was then displaced by sprinkling, but retained by the Greeks."

Augusti was an eminent Lutheran scholar, Professor in the University of Bonn, a thoroughly competent witness.

GIESELER—*Church Hist.*—"For the *sake of the sick* the rite of sprinkling was introduced."

Dr. Gieseler was a Lutheran, Professor in the University of Bonn.

KURTZ—*Church Hist.*—"Baptism was administered by *complete immersion.*"

Dr. Kurtz, a Professor in the University of Dorpat, is a trustworthy Lutheran witness.

VAN COLLEN—*Hist. of Doctrines.*—"Immersion in water was general *until the thirteenth century.*"

WINER—*Christian Antiquities.*—"Affusion was at first applied only to the sick, but was gradually introduced for others after the seventh century, and in the *thirteenth became* the prevailing practice in the West."

Who can refute these Lutheran historians?

Dr. Brenner—*Hist. Bapt.*—"*Thirteen hundred years* was baptism generally . . . . performed by the *immersion of the person under water*; and only in extraordinary cases was sprinkling or affusion permitted. These latter methods of baptism were called in question, and even prohibited."

Bower—*Hist. of Popes.*—"Baptism by *immersion* was, undoubtedly, the apostolical practice, and was never dispensed with by the Church except in cases of sickness."

Bishop Bossuet—*Stennet ad Russen.*—"We are able to make it appear, by the acts of Councils, and by ancient rituals, that *for thirteen hundred years* baptism was thus administered (by immersion) throughout the whole Church, as far as possible."

Stackhouse—*History Bible.*—"We nowhere read in the Scripture of any one being baptized but by *immersion*, and several authors have proved, from the acts of Councils and ancient rituals, that this manner of immersion continued, as much as possible, to be used for *thirteen hundred years* after Christ."

Dr. Schaff—*Hist. Apostolic Church.*—"Immersion, and not sprinkling, was unquestionably the original, normal form. This is shown by the very meaning of the Greek words *baptizo, baptisma*, and the analogy of the baptism of John, which was performed in the Jordan (*en*), Matt. iii. 6; compare with 16; also *eis to Jordanen* (into the Jordan), Mark i. 9. Furthermore by the New Testament comparisons of baptism with the passage through the Red Sea (1 Cor. x. 2); with the flood (1 Pet. iii. 21): with a bath (Eph. v. 26, Titus iii. 5); with a burial and resurrection (Rom. vi. 4, Col. ii. 12); and, finally, by the general usage of ecclesiastical antiquity, *which was always immersion*, as it is to this day in the Oriental and also in the Græco-Russian Churches, pouring and sprinkling being substituted only in cases of urgent necessity, such as sickness and approaching death."

Dr. Schaff is a Presbyterian, and one of the most eminent of the scholars and the writers of this age. He is a thoroughly competent witness, and his testimony is worthy the careful study of every lover of the truth.

VENEMA—*Eccles. Hist.*—"It is without controversy that baptism, in the primitive Church, was administered by *immersion into water*, and not by sprinkling, seeing that John is said to have baptized in Jordan, and where there was much water, as Christ also did, by his disciples, in the neighborhood of those places. Philip, going down into the water, baptized the eunuch."

HAGENBACH—*Hist. Christian Church.*—"That baptism, in the beginning, was administered in the open air, in rivers and pools, or that it was by *immersion*, we know from the narratives in the New Testament. In later times there were prepared great baptismal fonts or chapels.

The person to be baptized descended several steps into the reservoir of water, and then the *whole body was immersed under the water.*"

WADDINGTON—*Church Hist.*—"The sacraments of the primitive Church were two—that of baptism and the Lord's Supper. The *ceremony of immersion*, the oldest form of baptism, was performed in the name of the three persons of the Trinity."

COLEMAN—*Ancient Hist.*—"In the primitive Church immersion was undeniably the common mode of baptism. This fact is so well established that it were needless to adduce authorities in proof of it. It is a great mistake to suppose that baptism by immersion was discontinued when infant baptism became generally prevalent. The practice of immersion continued *even unto the thirteenth or fourteenth century*. Indeed, it has never been formally abandoned, but is still the mode of administering infant baptism in the Greek Church and in several other Churches."

DR. WALL—*Hist. Infant Bapt.*—"This (immersion) is so plain and clear by an infinite number of passages, *that one can not but pity the weak endeavors of such pedobaptists as would maintain the negative of it.* So we ought to disown and show a dislike of the profane scoffs which some people give to the English anti-pedobaptists, merely for the use of dipping, when it was, in all probability, the way by which our blessed Savior, and for certain was the most usual and ordinary way by which the ancient Christians, did receive their baptism. It is a great want of prudence, as well as of honesty, to refuse to grant to an adversary what is certainly true, and may be proved so. It creates a jealousy of all the rest that one says. The custom of the Christians in the near succeeding times (to the apostles), being more largely and particularly delivered in books, is known to have been generally or ordinarily a total immersion.

"France seems to have been the first country in the world where baptism by affusion was used ordinarily to persons in health, and in the public way of administering it. It being allowed (in England) to weak children (though strong enough to be brought to Christ) to be baptized by affusion, many ladies and gentlemen first, and then by degrees the common people, would obtain the favor of the priest to have their children pass for weak children, too tender to endure dipping in water; especially (as Mr. Walker observes) if some instances really were, or were but fancied or framed, of some child taking hurt by it. And another thing that had a greater influence than this was that many of our English divines and other people had, during Queen Mary's bloody reign (from 1553 to 1558), fled to Germany, Switzerland, etc., and, coming back in Queen Elizabeth's time, they brought with them a great love to the customs of those Protestant Churches wherein they had sojourned; and especially the authority of Calvin, and the rules he had established at Geneva, had a mighty influence on a great number of our people about that time. Now Calvin had not only given his dictum in his Institutes that the difference is of no moment whether he that is baptized be dipped all over, and if so, whether thrice or once, or whether he be *only wetted* with the water poured on him, but he had also drawn up for the use of his church at Geneva (and afterward published to the world), a form of administering the sacraments, where, when he comes to order the act of baptizing, he words it thus: 'Then the minister of baptism pours water on the infant, saying, I baptize thee,' etc. There had been, as I said, some Synods in some dioceses in France that had spoken of affusion without mentioning immersion at all, that being the common practice; but for an office of liturgy of any church, this is, I believe, the first in the world that prescribes affusion absolutely.

"This General Assembly (Westminster, 1643), could not remember that fonts to be baptized in had been always used by the primitive Christians long before the beginning of Popery, and ever since churches were built; but that sprinkling, for the common use of baptizing, was really introduced (in France first, and then in the Popish countries) in times of Popery; and that accordingly all those countries in which the usurped power of the Pope is, or has been formerly owned, have left off dipping of children in the font, but that all other countries in the world (which had never regarded his authority) do still use it; and that basins, except in cases of necessity, were never used by Papists, nor any other Christians whatsoever, till by themselves. . . . So parallel to the rest of their reformation, *they reformed the font into a basin.*"

BISHOP SMITH—*Hist. Bapt.*—"We have only to go back six or eight hundred years, and *immersion was the only mode*, except in the case of the few baptized on their beds at the real or supposed approach of death. . . . Immersion was not only universal six or eight hundred years ago, but it was primitive and apostolic. . . . The bowl and sprinkling are strictly Genevan in their origin; that is, they were introduced by Calvin at Geneva."

DR. GEO. GREGORY—*Hist. Church.*—"The initiatory right of baptism (in the first century) was publicly performed by immersing the whole body."

BINGHAM—*Origines*—"As this (dipping) was the original, apostolical practice so it continued the *universal* practice of the Church for many ages."

DR. CAVE.—*Primitive Christianity.*—"The party to be baptized was wholly immersed, or put under water, whereby they did more notably and significantly express the three great ends and effects of baptism."

MAGDEBURG CENT.—"They (the apostles) baptized only adults. As to the baptism of infants, we have no example. As to the manner of baptizing, it was by *dipping* or plunging into the water."

DR. GEO. CHRISTIAN KNAPP—*Christian Theology.*—"*To baptisma* from *baptizein*, which properly signifies *to immerse* (like the German *Taufen*) *to dip in, to wash,* (by immersion). *Immersion* is peculiarly agreeable to the institution of Christ and to the practice of the Apostolical Church, and so even John baptized, and immersion remained common a long time after; except that in the third century, or perhaps earlier, the baptism of the sick (*baptisma clinicorum*) was performed by sprinkling or affusion. Still, some would not acknowledge this to be true baptism, and controversy arose concerning it, so unheard of was it at that time to baptize by simple affusion. Cyprian first defended baptism by sprinkling, when necessity called for it, but cautiously and with much limitation. By degrees, however, this mode of baptism became more customary, probably because it was found more convenient. Especially was this the case after the seventh century and in the Western Church, but it did not become universal until the commencement of the fourteenth century."

This witness was one of the most popular of modern Lutheran theologians. His *Lectures on Theology*, from which I copy this passage, was translated by Dr. Leonard Woods, Jr., President of Bowdoin College. Twelve years ago, the work had reached the twentieth edition.

DR. WHITBY.—"*Immersion* was religiously

CONCESSIONS OF PEDOBAPTIST WRITERS. 103

observed by all Christians for *thirteen centuries*, and was approved by the Church of England. And since the change of it into sprinkling *was made without any allowance from the Author of the institution*, or any license from any Council of the Church (of England), being that which the Romanist still urgeth to justify his refusal of the cup to the laity, it were to be wished that this custom (immersion) might be again of general use."

Dr. Whitby belonged to the Church of England.

DR. GEIKE.—" With the call to repent, John united a significant rite for all who were willing to own their sins and promise amendment of life. It was the new and striking requirement of baptism *which John had been sent by divine appointment to introduce.*

"The Mosaic ritual had indeed required washings and purifications, but they were mostly personal acts for cleansing from ceremonial defilements, and were repeated as often as new uncleanness demanded. But baptism was performed only once, and those who sought it had to receive it from the hands of John. The old rites and requirements of the Pharisees would not content him. A new symbol was needed, striking enough to express the vastness of the change he demanded and to form its fit beginning, and yet simple enough to be easily applied to the whole people, for all alike needed to break with the past and to

enter upon the life of spiritual effort he proclaimed. . . . . Washing had been in all ages used as a religious symbol and significant rite. Naaman's leprosy had been cleansed away in the waters of the Jordan. The priests in the temple practiced constant ablutions, and others were required daily from the people at large, to remove ceremonial impurity. David had prayed 'Wash me from mine iniquity.' Isaiah had cried, 'Wash you, make you clean, put away the evil of your doings.' Ezekiel had told his countrymen to 'Wash their hearts from wickedness.' . . . . Ablution in the East is indeed, of itself, almost a religious duty. The dust and heat weigh upon the spirits and heart like a load; its removal is refreshment and happiness. It was, hence, nearly impossible to see a *convert go down into a stream, travel-worn and soiled with dust, and, after disappearing for a moment, emerge, pure and fresh,* without feeling that the symbol suited and interpreted a strong craving of the human heart. It was no formal rite with John. . . .
'He was a good man,' says Josephus, 'and urged the Jews who were willing to live worthily, and to show uprightness one to another, and piety toward God, to be baptized.' For baptism was approved of by him, not as a means of obtaining pardon for some sins only, but for the purity of the whole body, when the soul had been cleansed beforehand by righteousness.

"On baptism itself he set no mysterious

sacramental value. It was only water, a mere emblem of the purification required in the heart and life, and needed in an after baptism of the Holy Spirit. No one could receive it until he had proved his sincerity by an humble, public confession of his sins. Baptism then became a moral vow, to show, by a better life, that the change of heart was genuine.

"Bathing in the Jordan had been a sacred symbol, at least since the days of Naaman, but *immersion* by one like John, with strict and humbling confession of sin, sacred vows of amendment, and hope of forgiveness, if they proved lasting, and all this, in preparation for the Messiah, was something *wholly new* in Israel. It marked, in a most striking way, the wonderful moral revolution which had taken place in the hearts of the people. If, as a school of the rabbis contend, it was even then the custom to baptize proselytes on their forsaking heathenism and seeking admission to the communion of Israel, the attitude of John toward the nation was even startling, and their submission to the rite a still greater proof of his power over the popular mind. In this case it was no less than the treatment of Israel as if it had become heathen, and needed to seek entrance again, on no higher footing than a Gentile convert, to the privileges it had lost.

"Wholly self-oblivious, tainted by no stain of human pride, self-consciousness or low ambition, John had felt it no usurpation to constitute himself the messenger predicted by Malachi, 'sent to prepare the way of the Lord.' Nor was his preaching more than an expansion of the prophet's words, that 'the Lord whom ye seek shall suddenly come to his temple, even the Messenger of the Covenant whom ye delight in.' He had received the commission from no human lips, but had been set apart to it from above before his birth. Filled with the grandeur of his mission, nothing arrested him nor turned him aside.

"The crowds saw in him the most unbending strength, united with the most complete self-sacrifice; a type of grand fidelity to God and his truth and of the lowliest self-denial. The sorrows and hopes of Israel seemed to shine out of his eyes—bright with the inspiration of his soul, but sad with the greatness of his work—as he summoned the crowds to repentance, alarmed them by words of terror, or led them in groups to the Jordan *and immersed each singly in its waters*, after earnest and full confession of their sins."

Hear this witness still further:

"John resisted no longer, and, leading Jesus into the stream, the rite was performed. Can we question that such an act was a crisis in the life of our Lord? His perfect manhood, like that of other men, in all things except sin, forbids our doubting it. Holy and pure *before sinking under the waters, he must yet have risen from them* with the light of a higher glory in his countenance. His past life was closed; a new era had opened. Hitherto the humble villager, veiled from the world, he was henceforth the Messiah, openly working among men. It was the true moment of his entrance on a new life. Past years had been *buried* in the waters of the Jordan. He entered them as Jesus the Son of man; he *rose from them* the Christ, the Son of God."—"*Life of Christ.*"

This writer, Dr. Geikie, is a most eminent Christian scholar and divine. He is a pedobaptist, and can not be accused of partiality toward the Baptists. He is certainly a most competent witness as to the mode of baptism, and his testimony is very full and explicit. He tells us John's baptism was immersion; that he immersed each convert singly, after confession of sin; that our Lord, when baptized, *sank under the waters of the Jordan* and *rose from them.* Can any sane man believe that our Lord, in commanding baptism, enjoined any different *act* than the sort of one used in his own baptism and described by the very same word? Clearly not. The word employed to name it is the same, and therefore the act itself must be the same—immersion.

Now, my dear brother, tell me what I am to do with the testimony of these *twenty-four* pedobaptist witnesses. It establishes the historic fact that immersion is the apostolic baptism, and that sprinkling and infant baptism are the inventions of men. In the face of such evidence, from so many most credible witnesses, how can I resume those pedobaptist practices? Pedobaptist historians of the highest rank being judges, our Baptist practice of the *immersion* of *professed believers only*, as the scriptural baptism, is identical with the practice of the apostles, and required by the command of our Lord himself. How, then, can I cease this practice without disobedience to Christ and a willful departure from apostolic precedent? And how can I venture on such disobedience without incurring guilt? And could such disobedience fail to grieve my Lord? You can not fail to note my peculiar situation. In the kindness of your heart, you beg me to come back into the pedobaptist fold; but your own most eminent historians with one voice testify that the Baptist practice is apostolic, and pedobaptism an invention of subsequent ages, contrary to the example and command of our Lord and to the practice of his apostles. They are competent witnesses, and their testimony is very full and conclusive. Now all this—corroborated by a great cloud of other pedobaptist witnesses, men of the greatest eminence, men whose learning and truthfulness no one will deny—

puts me in a most peculiar predicament. It pens me up, as it were, where I am.

And it does more than that. It throws me into a brown study. In the light of these multiplied testimonies, I can not quite understand why you do not come over to the Baptists. You profess to love our Lord, and to make his Word the rule of your life. Then why not obey that Word in respect to baptism, as well as in other things? If baptism is a small matter, why not obey in small things? As ever, yours, ———.

VI.

TESTIMONY OF THE ENCYCLOPEDIAS.

"Forever, O Lord, thy word is settled in heaven."
—Psalmist.

My Dear Brother:—Is it not a singular fact that those ponderous tomes, the encyclopedias, are, universally, swift witnesses against pedobaptist practices? Of course, I refer to those great literary standard works which are prepared not in the interest of any sect, but for the conservation of impartial, unbending truth alone. With rare exceptions they are the product of the ripest scholarship and the most thorough research of the age, written by a host of the most talented men, who are selected from widely separated regions, from the various professions, and without the slightest regard to denominational lines, on the score of fitness. And they embody, in a condensed form, the best results of the widest investigation and the latest discoveries by the most eminent students in all the various fields of observation and of thought.

They are neither controversial nor partial, neither Baptist nor pedobaptist, but, like every good dictionary, independent, concise, and, as far as possible to the most careful and painstaking erudition, correct. Generally, if not always, it has so happened hitherto that they have been edited and published by men who are pedobaptists, chiefly, I suppose, because, in "the present distress," our Baptist friends are comparatively in the minority, and have too much other work on hand to permit them to engage largely in encyclopedia-making—a state of things likely to change by and by.

But this fact, that they are usually, if not in every instance, controlled by pedobaptist editors and publishers, adds great weight to that other fact to which I called your attention at the beginning of this letter—that they are, universally, swift witnesses against pedobaptist practices. Strange, isn't it, that they don't sometimes lean the other way? One would think that if the pedobaptists were right, these great reservoirs of knowledge would be full of evidences, incidental and direct, in support of their own claims. Indeed, granting they are right, one can not imagine how the great encyclopedias could be so made up as even to obscure that fact in the least degree, especially under the management of men friendly to their peculiar views and usages. And yet there stands the fact that the encyclopedias, sent forth by men of the highest character, as repositories of incontestable truth for the enlightenment of mankind, bear distinct testimony against them.

ENCYCLOPEDIA BRITANNICA—*Art. Baptism.*— "Christian baptism is the sacrament by which a person is initiated into the Christian Church. The word is derived from the Greek *baptizo*, the frequentative form of *bapto, to dip, or wash.* The usual way of performing the ceremony was by *immersion.* In the case of sick persons (*clinici*) the minister was allowed to baptize by pouring water upon the head, or by sprinkling. In the early Church '*clinical*' baptism, as it was called, was only permitted in cases of necessity, but the practice of baptism by sprinkling gradually came in, in spite of the opposition of councils and hostile decrees. The Council of Ravenna, in 1311, was the first Council of the Church which legalized baptism by sprinkling, by leaving it to the choice of the officiating minister."

ENCYCLOPEDIA AMERICANA—*Art. Baptism.*— "Baptism (that is, *dipping, immersing*, from the Greek *baptizo*) was usual with the Jews even before Christ. In the time of the apostles the form of baptism was very simple.

The person to be baptized *was dipped in a river*, or *vessel*, with the words which Christ had ordered, and, to express more fully his change of character, generally adopted a new name."

METROPOLITAN ENCYCLOPEDIA—*Art. Bapt.*—"We readily admit that the *literal meaning* of the word baptism is *immersion*, and that the desire of resorting again to the most ancient practice of the Church of *immersing the body*, which has been expressed by many divines, is well worthy of being considered."

PENNY CYCLOPEDIA—*Art. Bapt.*—"The manner in which it (baptism) was performed appears to have been at first by *immersion*."

CHAMBERS'S ENCYCLOPEDIA—*Art. Bapt.*—"It is, however, indisputable that, in the primitive Church, the ordinary mode of baptism was by *immersion*, in order to which baptisteries began to be erected in the third, perhaps in the second century, and the sexes were usually baptized apart. But baptism was administered to sick persons by sprinkling, although doubts as to the complete efficacy of this *clinic* (sick) baptism were evidently prevalent in the time of Cyprian, in the middle of the third century. Baptism by sprinkling gradually became more prevalent, but the dispute concerning the mode of baptism became one of the irreconcilable differences between the *Eastern* and the *Western* churches, the former generally adhering to the practice of immersion, while the latter adopted the mere pouring of water on the head, or sprinkling on the face; which practice has generally prevailed since the *thirteenth century*, but not universally, for it was the ordinary practice in England, before the Reformation, *to immerse* infants, and the *fonts* in the churches were made large enough for this purpose. This continued also to be the practice until the reign of Elizabeth, and the change which then took place is ascribed to the English divines who had sought refuge in Geneva and other places on the continent during the reign of Mary.

"To this day the rubric of the Church of England requires that, if the godfathers and godmothers 'shall certify that the child may well endure it, the officiating priest shall dip it in the water discreetly and warily,' and it is only 'if they shall certify that the child is weak,' that 'it shall suffice to pour water upon it;' which, however, or sprinkling, is now the ordinary practice."

Surely this is strong testimony from a very high source, such as only the behests of undeniable truth could have extorted from its author.

EDINBURGH ENCYCLOPEDIA—*Art. Baptism.*— "The first law to sanction *aspersion* as a mode of baptism was by Pope Stephen II., A. D. 753. But it was not till the year 1311 that a Council, held at Ravenna, declared immersion or sprinkling to be indifferent. In this country, however (Scotland), sprinkling was never practiced in ordinary cases till after the Reformation; and in England, even in the reign of Edward VI., immersion was commonly observed. These Scottish exiles, who had renounced the authority of the Pope, implicitly acknowledged the authority of Calvin, and, returning to their own country, with John Knox at their head, in 1559 established sprinkling in Scotland.

"From Scotland it made its way into England in the reign of Elizabeth, but was not authorized by the Established Church. In the Assembly of Divines, held at Westminster in 1643, it was keenly debated whether immersion or sprinkling should be adopted: *twenty-five voted for sprinkling*, and *twenty-four for immersion*; and even that small majority was attained at the earnest request of Dr. Lightfoot, who had acquired great influence in the Assembly."

Art. *Baptisteries*. — "Baptisteries were anciently very capacious, because, as Dr. Cote observes, the stated times of baptism returning but seldom, there were usually great multitudes to be baptized at the same time, and then the manner of baptizing by immersion, or dipping under water, made it necessary to have a large font."

NATIONAL CYCLOPEDIA—*Art. Bapt.* — "The manner in which the rite was performed appears to have been at first by *complete immersion*."

REES'S CYCLOPEDIA—*Art. Bapt.*—"In primitive times this ceremony was performed by *immersion.*"

BRAND'S CYCLOPEDIA—*Art. Bapt.*—"Baptism was originally administered by *immersion*, which act is thought by some necessary to the sacrament."

ENCYCLOPEDIA ECCLESIASTICA—*Art. Bapt.*—"Whatever weight, however, may be in these reasons, as a defense for the present practice of sprinkling, it is evident that during the first ages of the Church, and for many centuries afterward, the practice of *immersion* prevailed."

SCHAFF-HERZOG ENCYCLOPEDIA OF RELIGIOUS KNOWLEDGE—*Art. Bapt.*—"In the primitive Church, baptism was by *immersion*, except in the case of the sick (*clinic* baptism), who were baptized by pouring, or sprinkling. These latter were often regarded as not properly baptized, either because they had not completed their catechumenate, or the symbolism of the rite was not fully observed, or because of the small amount of water necessarily used. [The twelfth canon of the Council of Neo-Cæsarea (314-325) is: 'Whoever has received *clinic* baptism (through his own fault) can not become a priest, because he professed his faith under pressure (fear of death), and not from deliberate choice, unless he greatly excel afterward in zeal and faith, or there is a deficiency of other eligible men.'—Hefele, *Conciliengeschichte*, Vol. I., Sec. 17, first edition.] In A. D. 816, the Council of Calcuith (Chelsea, in England) forbade the priests to pour water upon the infants' heads, but ordered to immerse them. Hefele (Vol. IV., Sec. 414): 'The Council of Nemours (1284) limited sprinkling to cases of necessity,' and Thomas Aquinas (*Summa Theologica*, ¶III., Qu. 66., Art 7, *De Baptismo*) says: 'Although it may be safer to baptize by immersion, yet pouring and sprinkling are also allowable.' The Council of Ravenna (1311) was the first to allow a choice between sprinkling and immersion (eleventh canon, Hefele, Vol. VI., Sec. 699); but, at an earlier date (1287), the canons of the Council of the Liege Bishop John prescribe the way in which the sprinkling of children should be performed. *The practice first came into common use at the end of the thirteenth century*, and was favored by the growing rarity of adult baptism. It is the present practice of the Roman Church; but in the Greek Church immersion is insisted on as essential. Luther sided with the immersionists, described the baptismal act as an immersion, and derived *Taufe* (German for 'baptism') from *tief* ('deep'), because what one baptized, he sank *tief* in the water."

KITTO'S ENCYCLOPEDIA OF BIBLICAL LITERATURE—*Art. Bapt.*—"Infant baptism was established neither by Christ nor the apostles. In all places where we find the necessity of baptism notified, either in a dogmatic or historical point of view, it is evident that it was only meant for those who were capable of comprehending the word preached, and of being converted to Christ by an act of their own will.

A pretty sure testimony of its non-existence in the apostolic age may be inferred from 1 Cor. vii. 14, since Paul would certainly have referred to the baptism of the children for their holiness. (Compare Neander, 'History of Planting,' page 206.) But even in later times, several teachers of the Church, such as Tertullian (*De Bapt.*, 18) and others, reject the custom; indeed, his Church in general (that of North Africa) adhered longer than the others to the primitive regulations. Even when the baptism of children was already theoretically derived from the apostles, its practice was nevertheless, for a long time, confined to a mature age.

"In support of the contrary opinion, the advocates in former ages (now hardly any) used to appeal to Matt. xix. 14; but their strongest argument in its favor is the regulation of baptizing all the members of a house and family (1 Cor. xvi. 15, Acts xvi. 33, and Acts xviii. 8.) In none of these instances has it been proved that there were little children among them; but even supposing that there were, there was no necessity for excluding them from baptism in plain words, since such exclusion was understood as a matter of course.

"Many circumstances conspired early to introduce the practice of infant baptizing. The confusion between the outward and inward conditions of baptism, and the magical effect that was imputed to it; confusion of thought about the visible and invisible church, condemning all those who did not belong to the former; the doctrine of the natural corruption of man, so closely connected with the preceding; and finally, the desire of distinguishing Christian children from the Jewish and heathen, and of commending them more effectually to the care of the Christian community;—all these circumstances, and many more, have contributed to the introduction of infant baptism at a very early period."—*Prof. J. Jacobi.*

"As the topic of baptism seemed to be well exhausted in this country, the editor thought that some freshness of effect might be produced by presenting the subject to the reader from a German point of view. The article was therefore offered to Dr. Neander, the Church Historian and Professor of Theology in the University of Berlin. His multiplied preëngagements, however, induced him, with the editor's consent, to consign the subject to Rev. J. Jacobi, of the same University; and in due time the MS. of the present article arrived, accompanied by the following note from Dr. Neander, to whose inspection it had previously been submitted by the author:

"'As my other labors would not permit me to work out the article (on baptism) for the Cyclopedia of Biblical Literature, I requested a dear friend, J. Jacobi, to undertake it, who, by his knowledge and critical talents, is fully qualified for the task, and whose theological principles are in unison with my own.

"'A. NEANDER.'"
—*Editorial Note, Kitto's Cyclopedia, Art. Baptism.*

Now, my dear brother, if you will scan these testimonies from *twelve* standard encyclopedias, you will not fail to find in them "food for thought" that will prove to be at least interesting, if not cheering to you. With one voice they testify that immersion is the primitive apostolic baptism. And they show conclusively that sprinkling is of a later date—a contrivance of men that originated in a false idea respecting the importance of baptism—moving those whom it controlled to devise a sort of compromise with the Lord by the substitution of a sort of *bed-bath* for that full immersion which constituted the true and the only authorized baptism, in the hope that the Lord would accept it, since a full act of baptism had become impossible.

And they trace the gradual growth of that *bed-bath* substitute for baptism in the public favor, until, after the lapse of more than one thousand years from its first appearance, it came, in some quarters of the Roman Catholic Church, to be very generally accepted in place of the true baptism. And then they show the lamentable spectacle of the great leaders of the early Protestantism of Europe consenting to continue the use of this conceded innovation. They show us how the great reputation of

Calvin, Knox and Lightfoot gave it currency, until it became the general practice in Scotland and in England. And we are assured by these great authorities that, as this contrivance of men grew in popularity, it steadily diminished in volume, until, from a full bed-bath, it shrank away into a mere moistening of a bit of the forehead by a few drops of water from the wetted tips of two or three fingers of the priestly hand—a queer sort of sprinkling, with the sprinkling left out—such as the great mass of pedobaptist ministers gravely persist in using to this day. And one of these witnesses, whose testimony no man disputes, tells us how this shrunken contrivance was imposed upon the good people of old England by the Westminster Assembly, about the middle of the seventeenth century, by a vote of *twenty-five* to *twenty-four*, and the witness adds the undeniable but rather humiliating fact, that "Even that small majority was attained at the earnest request of Dr. Lightfoot, who had acquired great influence in the Assembly."

There you have it in a very few words. The authority of Christ in his own ordinance set aside, first by North African superstition; then by Roman Catholic audacity fully supplanted in Catholic lands, and, at last, superseded among English-speaking Protestants *by the vote of one man.*

And parallel with this great change, these witnesses establish the fact of another change respecting the same ordinance, equally unwarranted and even more destructive in its influence upon the Christian world—the introduction and establishment of infant baptism. Beginning about the same time as the *bed-bath*, arising out of the same superstitious notions of the virtue of baptism as an indispensable medium of the grace of eternal life, and sustained by the weight of great names, by appeals to the tender affections of parents toward their helpless babes, favored by the growing formalism and the deepening ignorance and credulity of the masses of the people, and, at length, adopted and rigidly enforced by the civil and ecclesiastical powers by means of the dreaded excommunication, and by the still more potent agency of the prison, the faggot and the sword, it was made effective and well-nigh universal many hundreds of years before its twin sister, sprinkling, attained to general acceptance and popular favor.

And this change, made by men and perpetuated by men against the example and authority of Christ and his apostles, made possible the usurpations, corruptions and tyranny of the Papacy, and of all State and Church establishments, by introducing the corrupt world into the Church *en masse*, until a large part of Christendom came to be—what large sections of it are even to this day—merely a baptized paganism, as you may see in Mexico, Spain, Italy, Austria, France, Russia, and many other nominally Christian countries. And these two great and deadly innovations are to-day in use, honored, practiced, and, as far as possible, defended, in all pedobaptist churches.

Now, my dear brother, consider my dilemma. If I remain a Baptist, I am sure to be denounced by my pedobaptist friends as a narrow-minded bigot, as opposed to the broad, liberal, intelligent and progressive spirit of the age; and unless you have an immense amount of grace, *you* will join in the hue and cry against me, especially if I am—what I ought to be—an earnest, wide-awake, decided Baptist. But, on the other hand, if I cease to be a Baptist and accept your kind invitation to return to my old pedobaptist home, I will, thereby, cease to obey Christ in the most solemn acts of worship—in the use of his ordinances—and at once begin the use of mere human substitutes for the things he has commanded. And I could not now plead ignorance as an excuse for such strange disobedience to the Master, for these great encyclopedic witnesses, were there no others, would condemn me. If they stood alone, their testimony is so clear and so formidable that I am quite sure it could never be set aside. But, as you are well aware, they are not alone; they constitute only one of many great bands of witnesses, each of which is, of itself, convincing and incontrovertible.

Why just think of it; they might well be called *legion*, for they are many—a great host—and their ranks are rapidly growing larger and more respectable all the time. If I should come back to you, I could no more refute these pedobaptist witnesses against pedobaptist practices than I could *effectually* "call spirits from the vasty deep." I would be as powerless, in that respect, as you are, and my only hope of any peace would be in shutting my eyes and closing my ears, so that I might not see nor hear these troublesome testimonies against us from our own camp. But even that painful plan would surely fail; for the light and the truth that have already gained an entrance into my mind could not be thrust out by any process that I know of, and the voice of conscience would certainly torment me all the time. Then how could I go at it to defend pedobaptist practices under such circumstances? Honestly, my brother, I do not believe I could do it. I do not claim to excel other disciples of the Master in piety and goodness, but to stand up before a congregation on the Lord's day, or on any other day, and gravely tell them that sprinkling is baptism, and that infant baptism is scriptural, requires a degree of egotistic boldness and a recklessness of "putting things" to which I confess I am not at all equal. Therefore, unless you can devise some plan to get rid of these encyclopedians and the other clouds of pedobaptist witnesses against your practice, I shall be obliged to decline your generous invitation.

But with due deference to your talent and learning, I do not anticipate anything of that sort. Even very able men can not accomplish the impossible. Facts are not only "stubborn things," but, when well-defined, they are stronger than any man's rhetoric. I know your wit and genius and logical acumen are of no mean order, but the task—"to make the worse appear the better reason"—in this case is appalling. Like towering mountain peaks the adverse facts rise up on every side, and the fogs have disappeared to such a degree that longer concealment of them is quite beyond the skill of any man.

Indeed, I am not sure that you may not be in a mood to give up the unequal contest and come over to the Baptists. Should you conclude to do so, you will lose your harassing doubts and gain a certainty of the approval of the Master that will be a perpetual joy.

   Fraternally yours, ———.

VII.

THE SYMBOLISM OF BAPTISM.

"*Therefore we are buried with him by baptism into death.*"—PAUL.

MY DEAR BROTHER:—The symbolism of baptism very clearly indicates its external form. Indeed, the symbolism is in the form and inseparable from it. Change the form, and you at once destroy the symbolism. The ordinance of the Lord's Supper, when duly observed according to the manner of its institution, is an eloquent symbol of his death, and of the benefits derived from it by the believer. It speaks of a body broken for us, and of blood shed for us, and of the benefits of both appropriated by faith, cleansing from sin, and sustaining the renewed, spiritual life—the life of God in the soul—as bread supports the physical life.

But now omit the breaking of the bread, and take away the cup, and what remains?

The sacrificial element of the symbolism is eliminated. Under the emblem of the bread eaten, our dependence on Christ is symbolized; but it is not the Christ crucified. The new symbol is fully met and all its demands are satisfied, when those who employ it accept the Christ as a teacher-sent from God, and adopt him as the model man, whose excellencies they will seek to imitate in developing their own characters—living by him in precisely the same sense in which the philosophic student lives by his master. Who needs to be told that this would be another gospel than the old apostolic one which was "the power of God unto salvation"—a gospel with neither cross, nor blood, nor life in it? And yet it is the indisputable teaching of the symbolism of the Supper, when the outward form of it has been changed in only these two particulars.

In a similar way must a change in the form of baptism affect the symbolic teaching of that ordinance. If you change the immersion into sprinkling, you have a symbolism of cleansing —that, and nothing more. If you inquire concerning the nature and extent of the cleansing, the modified ordinance is silent. If you ask by what means that cleansing is effected, the new ordinance is equally silent. It has but

THE SYMBOLISM OF BAPTISM. 129

one voice, and that tells of a cleansing, and gives no hint of the agency by which it is to be effected, nor of the thoroughness of it. In changing the form of the ordinance, you have changed and thereby destroyed its symbolism. If you doubt this, interrogate the ordinance in its original apostolic form—immersion.

To begin with, it symbolizes a cleansing, in the use of that cleansing element, water. But it does not stop there. *Submersion* beneath the baptismal waters can not mean less than an entire, complete cleansing of the whole person. Every part goes into the water, and beneath the surface of it, and that indicates that every part must be cleansed—not the head only, but the hands, the feet, the heart, as well.

But look carefully into the baptismal font. Do you not see therein more than a symbol of cleansing? What mean the descent of the candidate under the water and his ascent therefrom? Is it possible that an ordinance so peculiar, means nothing more than cleansing? Is there not, in the hiding of the baptized, for the moment, beneath the water, some special meaning? An inspired apostle treats it as a symbol of burial with Christ. He calls it "the likeness of his death." And the least that this can mean is, that it is something so related, in form, to death—something so associated with death—that it recalls the fact of death; and being done in the name of the Son, it brings before the mind his death.

And you will concede that there is in immersion a striking resemblance to a burial. There is, in the sinking out of sight, or, at least, beneath the water, as perfect a symbol of burial as human ingenuity can well imagine.

But only the dead are usually buried. Christ was not laid away out of sight of men, in Joseph's new tomb, until he was dead. We do not lay the bodies of our friends in the grave until they are dead. But when they are dead, the next thing in order is their burial; and this follows so certainly and so uniformly that a burial always speaks to us of death.

So the man who turns to Christ, abandons the old life of sin—becomes dead to it, and it to him—does it by virtue of the death of Christ, by which he becomes crucified to the world—and so, entering the baptismal bath, he is symbolically and solemnly "buried with him into death." The thing set forth by the baptismal burial is not the manner of the death, but the fact of it, and the efficacious cause of it. And then, very naturally, the rising out of the water becomes the symbol of the rising into the new life of Christ-following, through the power of the risen and glorified Christ.

So inspiration describes the symbolism of baptism—gives to each part of its divinely prescribed form a voice that no one can mistake. As a man descends into the water, he thereby proclaims himself dead to sin, dead to the old life, dead to it through the death of Christ; and, because thus dead, he will be buried with Christ. But death to sin implies a resurrection to holiness. So he rises up to a new life through the resurrection of Christ. As the death of Christ, "who was delivered for our offenses," wrought his death to sin, thereby fitting himself to be "buried with him," so the resurrection of Christ, "who rose again for our justification," wrought in him "newness of life," making him meet to rise with him into a life of Christ-likeness. So his symbolic burial is followed immediately by a symbolic resurrection. That this is the true and actual symbolism of baptism rests upon a solid basis— nothing less than the testimony of the great apostle to the Gentiles in the sixth chapter of Romans, and also in the second chapter of Colossians. No man in his senses can imagine, even for a moment, that any person is literally buried by baptism into death. Taken in such a sense, the statement in Rom. vi. 4, is an evident absurdity.

But not less absurd is it when construed as the statement of a spiritual burial by a spiritual baptism, or of a spiritual burial by a literal baptism. There is no allusion, in the entire passage, to a spiritual baptism. Such baptism is not the theme of the discussion, nor can it, in any way, be pressed into the discussion, either as an argument or as an illustration. The argument is a refutation of the proposition, "Let us continue in sin, that grace may abound"—a proposition that could not have emanated from those who had actually received the baptism of the Spirit. Yet those who are supposed to urge it, as a license of sinful living, are addressed as "baptized" persons, and from their own baptism is drawn a very powerful refutation of their error. They had been "baptized into Christ," and in that act had been also "baptized into his death." In fact, they had been "buried with him by baptism into death." All this points distinctly to a *literal* baptism, and recalls most forcibly the solemn professions made in that act, urging them as conclusive reasons why those who have been so baptized should live holy lives. In that solem transaction they had renounced the old life of sin, and had, in some way, declared themselves dead to it, engaging also to walk "in newness of life;" and these solemn vows and professions, in their baptism, bound them to a life of holiness, and the more so, that, in some way, they had been united together in the "likeness of his death" in that ordinance.

Now there is nothing in the "baptism of the Spirit" that tallies with this argument. That baptism does not "bury" men "into death." There is in it no shadow of the "likeness of his death." It quickens men who are already spiritually alive into an intensity of spiritual life and power not otherwise attainable by the best of men. Those who had received that baptism would need no argument to convince them that they should not "continue in sin, that grace may abound." Imagine Peter and John, the next day after Pentecost, saying, "Let us continue in sin, that grace may abound!"

Nor can the apostle, in Rom. vi. 4, intend to ascribe a *spiritual* burial to a *literal* baptism, for that were to clothe such baptism with a transforming power entirely foreign to it; a power to regenerate and save the soul, actually, "washing away the filth of the flesh," and making all the baptized "heirs of God and joint heirs with Jesus Christ." If the apostle means to tell us that by literal baptism men are spiritually, that is, actually, made "dead to sin," and alive with Christ, then in another place he should have written, "Therefore, being justified by *baptism*, we have peace with God," and in another place, "By grace are ye saved, through *baptism*," and in another, "The just shall live by *baptism*." And in that case, he should have omitted the sixth chapter of Romans entirely, since the things he there labors to establish must have been already secured beyond a peradventure, by the simpler process of baptism.

But evidently the apostle regarded baptism, not as a *saving*, but simply as a *professing* ordinance; and thence drew legitimate arguments, enforcing upon the baptized the imperative duty of making good in the life the solemn and beautiful vows of the baptismal font.

And this conclusion, which can not rationally be evaded by any careful biblical student, makes it evident that the baptism dwelt upon in the sixth chapter of Romans is that literal water baptism which our Lord established for all his disciples, to which those ancient brethren in Rome had submitted, and by which are set forth, figuratively, the death of the baptized to sin, and his consequent resurrection into a new, holy life through the death and resurrection of our Lord.

But this being admitted, we have in this symbolism a sure indication of the form of the apostolic baptism. Only an immersion could give the symbolism of a burial and a rising again. The son of a certain Presbyterian minister understood this matter very thoroughly. His father, leaving home to fill an appointment, told him to go and bury a goose which had just died. Returning home, the old gentleman saw the goose in the middle of the road, a little dust having been sprinkled over it. Calling his son, he said:

"Did I not tell you to bury that goose?"

"Yes, sir," was the prompt reply, "and I did bury it."

"Beware, sir," replied the father; "beware how you trifle with me. You did not *bury* that goose. You left it in the middle of the road, with a little dust sprinkled over it. Do you call that burying it?"

"Why, yes, sir," said the son; "I buried the goose by sprinkling, just as you bury the people in baptism by sprinkling. Isn't that the right way to bury things?"

"An old saw!" you say. Yes, so it is; but

a very sharp one, and so set that it cuts to the line. No ingenuity of man can make sprinkling fit into Rom. vi. 4. It suits neither the text nor the sense. Suppose we read it as you pedobaptists practice it; "Therefore, we are buried with him by *sprinkling* into death. Yet this reading, which is so absurd that no educated pedobaptist on earth would think of defending it, expresses precisely the incongruity of your practice. Why blame a boy for burying a goose by sprinkling, when hosts of grave divines are employed every day *burying* men, women and children in the same way? How can the boy be wrong if those divines are right?

The symbolism of baptism, as set forth by the apostle in Rom. vi. 4, is a great obstacle in the way of those who are determined to promote the practice of sprinkling, for the average man can not understand how it is that a mere wetting of the forehead can symbolize a burial, or how it can be in any sense a likeness of Christ's death. And, if left to himself, he is sure to conclude that the baptism to which the apostle alludes is an immersion; whence, in his judgment, it inevitably follows that the true apostolic baptism—that to which our Lord himself submitted—that which he commands his disciples to administer, and that which they did administer—is not a sprinkling but an immersion.

Hence the remarkable efforts of a very few modern pedobaptist writers to put a new interpretation upon the apostolic words, and thereby break their force, or, at least, in some measure, obscure their meaning. But these efforts are predestined failures. Coming at so late a day, and with a purpose so evidently partisan, and being in their very nature so contrary to the plain, unmistakable import of the inspired words, they can not deceive very many.

The great mass of pedobaptist writers frankly admit that the baptism mentioned in Rom. vi. 4, is immersion. Permit me to place before you a few samples from some of your best authors on this point. If you do not care to read them, you can skip over a few pages; but I advise you to examine them patiently and carefully, that you may have some notion of the mountains of evidence—undoubted pedobaptist evidence—over which I must wearily climb if I accept your kind invitation to return again to my old pedobaptist church home. These, and a host more, equally conclusive testimonies, seem to warn me away from your verdant, fields, with ill-concealed intimations that underneath their inviting slopes there are dangerous quicksands, which the wary pilgrim would do well carefully to avoid.

Or, if you like not similes so pastoral, they are so many glowing foot-lights, exposing the paint and tinselry and inventions of the play in which you so kindly invite me to join, and assuring me that a performance so entirely artistic and artificial can be neither wholesome nor enduring.

And really, I do not mind telling you that, sitting here before this great mass of brilliant foot-lights, I am rather glad that I am no longer behind those painted scenes. And I half believe that, in your heart, you will agree with me that the emptiness of the play is at times a severe trial to the Christian manhood of the actors. At all events, you must admit that there is something of weariness in being obliged to deal forever with mere shadows and contrivances, that, at the best, amount to nothing, while they tax your ingenuity and patience in the bootless task of patching, repairing and defending them.

Should this be, indeed, your sad plight, I know of no other remedy than to abandon at once the whole play, and hasten over to the solid verities of gospel truth and practice. And having myself tried this remedy, I can assure you that it is effective and comforting, giving one a sense of relief from harassing uncertainty, and a most comfortable and ever-growing conviction that the old way, to which one has newly come, is the divinely-ordained, and therefore the indisputably right and enduring way.

Before I proceed to lay before you some of the testimonies of eminent pedobaptist writers on the meaning of Rom. vi. 4, "*Therefore we are buried with him by baptism into death,*" etc., allow me to remind you that, if it be conceded that the baptism alluded to is that which the apostles practiced, and that it was an immersion, then sprinkling must of necessity be post-apostolic, and equally of necessity must it be unscriptural—an unprofitable and unwarranted invention of men.

Now please study these testimonies from some of your best authors, and either refute them, or give up your indefensible practices, and join us in the practice and in the defense of scriptural baptism and its correlated scriptural truth.

REV. ALBERT BARNES on Rom. vi. 4, "*Therefore we are buried,*" etc.—"It is altogether probable that the apostle, in this place, had allusion to the custom of baptizing by immersion. This can not, indeed, be *proved* so as to be liable to no objection, but I presume this is the idea which would strike the great mass of unprejudiced readers."—*Notes on Romans.*

REV. THOMAS CHALMERS, D. D., LL. D., on Rom. vi. 3, 4.—"The original meaning of the word baptism is immersion, and though we regard it as a point of indifferency whether the ordinance so named be performed in this way or by sprinkling, yet we doubt not that the prevalent style in the apostles' days was by an actual submerging of the whole body under water. We advert to this for the purpose of throwing light on the analogy that is instituted in these verses. Jesus Christ, by death, underwent this sort of baptism, even immersion under the surface of the ground, whence he soon emerged again by his resurrection. We, by being baptized into his death, are conceived to have made a similar translation. In the act of descending under the water of baptism, to have resigned an old life; and in the act of ascending, to emerge into a second or a new life, along the course of which it is our part to maintain a strenuous avoidance of that sin, which as good as expunged the being that we had formerly, and a strenuous prosecution of that holiness, which should begin with the first moment that we were ushered into our present being, and be perpetuated and make progress toward the perfection of full and ripened immortality."—*Lectures.*

ARCHBISHOP TILLOTSON.—"*Being buried with him in baptism, wherein also ye are risen with him through the faith of the operation of God, who hath raised him from the dead.*

"*Being buried with him in baptism.* For the full understanding of this expression we must have recourse to that parallel text (Rom. vi. 3–5), which will explain to us the meaning of this phrase: '*Know ye not that so many of us as were baptized into* JESUS CHRIST *were baptized into his death? Therefore we are buried with him by baptism into death: that like as* CHRIST *was raised up from the dead by the glory of the* FATHER, *even so we also should walk in newness of life. For if we have been planted together in the likeness of his death, we shall be also in the likeness of his resurrection.*' Where we see that *to be baptized into the death and resurrection of* CHRIST IS TO BE BAPTIZED INTO THE SIMILITUDE AND LIKENESS OF THEM; and the resemblance is this, that as CHRIST, being dead, was buried in the grave, and, after some stay in it, that is, for three days, he was raised again out of it, by the glorious power of God, to a new and heavenly life, being not long after taken up into heaven to live at the right hand of God; so Christians, when they were baptized, *were immersed into the water,* . . . . their bodies being covered all over with it; which is, therefore, called our being *buried in baptism into death*; and after some short stay under water, were raised or taken up again out of it, as if they had been recovered to a new life, by all which was spiritually signified our dying to sin, and being raised to a divine and heavenly life *through the faith of the operation of God*; that is, by that divine and supernatural power which raised up CHRIST from the dead. So that Christians from henceforth were to reckon themselves dead unto sin, but alive unto God, through JESUS CHRIST, as the apostle speaks (Rom. vi. 11)."—*Sermon on Resurrection of Christ.*

WHITEFIELD on Rom. vi. 3, 4.—"It is certain that in the words of our text there is an allusion to the manner of baptizing, which was by immersion."

JOHN WESLEY on Rom. vi. 4.—"The allusion is to the ancient manner of baptizing by immersion."—*Notes.*

BENSON on Rom. vi. 4, "*Buried with Christ by baptism.*"—"Alluding to the ancient manner of baptizing by immersion."—*Commentary.*

BLOOMFIELD on Rom. vi. 4.—"Here is a plain allusion to the ancient custom of baptizing by immersion, and I agree with *Koppe* and *Rosenmuller* that there is reason to regret that it should have been abandoned in most Christian churches, especially as it has so evident a reference to the mystic sense of baptism."

ADAM CLARK, D.D., on Rom. vi. 4.—"It is probable that the apostle here alludes to the mode of administering baptism by immersion, the whole body being put under water."

CONYBEARE AND HOWSON.—"It is needless to add that baptism was (unless in exceptional cases) administered by immersion, the convert being plunged beneath the surface of the water, to represent his death to the life of sin, and then raised from this momentary burial, to represent his resurrection to the life of righteousness. It must be a subject of regret that the general discontinuance of this original form of baptism (though, perhaps, necessary in our northern climates) has rendered obscure to popular apprehension some very important passages of Scripture."—*Life of St. Paul*, p. 439.

ULRICIUS ZWINGLIUS on Rom. vi. 3, 4.— "When ye were immersed into the water of baptism, ye were engrafted into the death of Christ: that is, the immersion of your body into water was a sign that ye ought to be engrafted into Christ and his death, that as Christ died and was buried, ye also may be dead to the flesh and the old man, that is, to yourselves."

PHILIP LIMBORCH—*On Baptism.*—"Baptism then consists in ablution, ór, rather, in the immersion of the whole body into water. For formerly those who were to be baptized were accustomed to be immersed with the whole body in water."

PROF. J. A. TURRETIN on Rom. vi. 3, 4.— "And, indeed, baptism was performed in that age (the apostolic age), and in those countries, by the immersion of the whole body into water."

DR. JAMES MCKNIGHT on Rom. vi. 4.— "Christ's baptism was not the baptism of repentance, for he never committed any sin. But he submitted to be baptized; that is, to be buried under the water by John, and then raised out again."

WILLIAM VAN EST on Rom. vi. 3.—"For immersion represents to us Christ's burial, and so also his death. For the tomb is a symbol of death, since none but the dead are buried. Moreover, the emersion which follows the immersion has a resemblance to a resurrection. We are, therefore, in baptism conformed not only to the death of Christ, as he has just said, but also to his burial and resurrection."

CANON FARRAR, D.D., F.R.S., "Life of St. Paul."—"The life of the Christian being hid with Christ in God, his death with Christ is a death to sin, his resurrection with Christ is a resurrection to life. *The dipping under the waters of baptism* is his union with Christ's death; *his rising out of the waters of baptism* is a resurrection with Christ and the birth to a new life." (Page 480).

PROF. F. GODET, D.D., on Rom. vi. 3, 4.— "Some take the word *baptize* in its literal sense of *bathing, plunging*, and understand, 'As many of you as were *plunged into Christ.*' . . 'One is not plunged into a name, but into water, *in relation to* (*eis*) a name—that is to say, to the new revelation of God expressed in a name.' Modern commentators are not at one on the question whether the apostle means to allude to the external form of the baptismal rite in the primitive church. It seems to us very probable that it is so, whether primitive baptism be regarded as a complete immersion, during which the baptized disappeared for a moment under water (which best corresponds to the figure of *burial*), or whether the baptized went down into the water up to his loins, and the baptizer poured the water with which he had filled the hollow of his hands over his head, so as to represent an immersion. The passage, Mark vii. 4, where the term *baptismos*, a *washing, bath, lustration, baptism* (Heb. vi. 2), is applied not only to the cleansing of *cups* and *utensils*, objects which may be plunged into water, but also to that of couches or divans, proves plainly that we can not insist on the sense of *plunging*, and consequently on the idea of total immersion, being attached to the term baptism. It is nevertheless true that in one or the other of these forms the going down into the water probably represents, in Paul's view, the moral burying of the baptized, and his issuing from the water his resurrection. The relation between the two facts of burial and baptism indicated by the apostle is this: Burial is the act which consummates the breaking of the last tie between man and his earthly life. This was likewise the meaning of our Lord's entombment. Similarly, by baptism there is publicly consummated the believer's breaking with the life of the present world and with his own natural life."

As to the baptism of couches and divans in Mark vii. 4, as an argument against the idea of a total immersion in baptism, as urged by this witness, it is necessary only to remind you that in the Revised Version of 1881, *there is neither couch, divan nor table in the text*, and so this old objection is utterly exploded, and that, too, substantially by pedobaptist authorities. And as to his notion of "the baptized" going "down into the water up to his loins, and the baptizer" pouring "the water with which he had filled the hollow of his hands over his head," you know perfectly well that it is only an idle fancy, used for a purpose—name'y, to help our author out of a very tight place.

H. A. W. MEYER, Th.D., on "Baptism of Jailer."—"This (*that* he led them to a neighboring water, perhaps in the court of the house, in which his baptism and that of his household was immediately completed), is confirmed by the fact that baptism took place by complete immersion, in opposition to Baumgarten, p. 515, who, transferring the performance of baptism to the house, finds here 'an approximation to the later custom of simplifying the ceremony,' according to which complete immersion did not take place. *Immersion was, in fact, quite an essential part of the symbolism of baptism.*" (Rom. vi.)—*Commentary on Acts, Note.*

The *italics* in the last sentence of this quotation are mine. This witness is certainly competent. Dr. Gloag calls him, "The greatest modern exegete." Dr. Ormiston says: "No name is entitled to take precedence of that of Meyer as a critical exegete, and it would be difficult to find one that equals him in the happy combination of superior learning with keen penetration, analytical power and clear, terse, vigorous expression. . . So impartial and candid is he, that he never allows his own peculiar views to color or distort his interpretations of the language of Scripture."

PHILIP SCHAFF, D.D., on Rom, vi. 4.—"All commentators of note (except *Stuart* and *Hodge*) expressly admit, or take it for granted that, in this verse, ... the ancient prevailing mode of baptism, by immersion and emersion, is implied as giving additional force to the idea of the going down of the old and the rising up of the new man. Bloomfield: 'There is a plain allusion to the ancient mode of baptism by immersion; on which, see Suicer's *Thes.* and Bingham's *Antiquities.*' Barnes: 'It is altogether probable that the apostle has allusion to the custom of baptizing by immersion.' Conybeare and Howson: 'This passage can not be understood, unless it be borne in mind that the primitive baptism was by immersion.' Webster and Wilkinson: 'Doubtless there is an allusion to immersion, as the usual mode of baptism, introduced to show that baptism symbolized our spiritual resurrection.' Compare also Bengel, Rückert, Tholuck, Meyer. The objection of Philippi (who, however, himself regards this allusion probable in verse 4), that, in this case, the apostles would have expressly mentioned the symbolic act, has no force in view of the daily practice of baptism."—*Commentary of Langé, Note.*

Here we have the testimony of a great host of witnesses, including Langé, Schaff, Bloomfield, Suicer, Bingham, Barnes, Conybeare, Howson, Webster, Wilkinson, Bengel, Rückert, Tholuck, Meyer, Philippi, and, indeed, *all commentators of note*—except two—that in Rom. vi. 4, the apostle alludes to baptism by immersion, calling it a burial with Christ, thereby "giving additional force to the idea of the going down of the old and the rising up of the new man." And this great array of witnesses establishes incontestably the fact that, in the days of the apostles, immersion was the prevailing mode of baptism. It was, then, these writers being judges, the *apostolic* mode, and therefore must have been the mode that our Lord instituted among his people by an explicit command, reinforced by his own amazing example. That it was the only mode then known in the churches of Christ is evident from two considerations: First, *all* who were baptized at all were *buried with him by baptism*, and if any were thus buried with him by immersion, then, of necessity, all were, since in a symbolical burial the one symbol is as needful for one as for another; and, second, the only explanation of the apostolic practice of immersion must be the command of the Master, and we can not conceive of the apostles as departing, in any case, from the thing commanded by our Lord.

Back of the authority of the apostles in their baptismal practice is the command of Christ; and both remain to this day unchanged. If, then, immersion was duty in apostolic times, it is also duty now, and he who substitutes for it some other way need not wonder if devout disciples of Christ demand his authority.

All that Dr. Schaff says about the use immersionists make of Rom. vi. 4, and about the necessity of an emersion following the immersion, together with his remarks about the substitution of immersion for baptism in the English Bible, is a sample of special pleading altogether unworthy his reputation as a great Christian scholar. No advocate of immersion thinks of urging Rom. vi. 4, *as a command to immerse*, but as containing *such an allusion to it as fairly demonstrates that immersion is the apos-*

tolic baptism, and, therefore, the baptism that our Lord requires; and the first of these facts being conceded by our pedobaptist friends generally, the second must also be admitted, or the apostles must be convicted of rank disobedience to Christ—a task which all good pedobaptists will be very slow to undertake.

As for the necessity of *emersion* as an essential part of apostolic baptism, I am quite sure that all Baptists are aware of it. In every case of apostolic baptism such *emersion* is emphasized, and that is one of the strong reasons for adhering to the Bible ordinance in its primitive form and simplicity.

Why Dr. Schaff should consider the term *immersion*, which is an exact equivalent of the Greek *baptizo*, a one-sided and secular word, is not exactly clear to ordinary mortals, unless it is because it would expose at a glance the utter unscripturalness of sprinkling. It is true that the substitution of immersion for baptism would give a view of the ordinance that might be truthfully described as a "negative," and a very decided one, of the practice of sprinkling. That "*baptism* and the corresponding verb" have long been "naturalized in the English language," no one denies; but, as Dr. Schaff is well aware, and as you also know perfectly well, *they did not bring with them their old Greek sense.* Practically, they are new English words, with new, technical English meanings—in no sense an equivalent of the Greek.

To compare the naturalization of *baptism* and *baptize* in English, with their new meanings, to the transfer of such words as *Christ, apostle, angel*, etc., which retain in English their old Greek sense, may be shrewd, but it is certainly neither scholarly nor transparently honest. It is a trick worthy a tenth-rate pettifogger, but sadly out of place in a stately commentary on the word of God. Its only use is to mislead ignorant or too-confiding readers by a statement *true in the letter of it, but false in the impression intended to be conveyed by it*. But thoughtful people who earnestly desire to know and do the truth will hardly be deceived so easily. They will be apt, however, to agree with the learned author of the article that, "*Immersion is, undoubtedly, a more expressive form than sprinkling,*" and finding in his own statements a very conclusive proof that it is also a more *legitimate* and *scriptural* form, they will be slow to accept a doubtful invention of men in its place. And they will not need a prophet to convince them that an innovation which, by changing the form of an ordinance, destroys its symbolic meaning, does very seriously impair the efficacy of that ordinance as a divinely-ordained object lesson in vital Christian truth. And it may be that, going a little further, they may conclude very wisely that "to obey is better than sacrifice," and so come to the safe and dutiful resolution to reject those indifferent and useless forms that men have contrived, and adhere firmly and reverently to those which divine wisdom has planned and divine authority has prescribed; and, you know that would make them straight-out, loyal Baptists. Such things have often occurred in the past, and they are occuring now, and doubtless they will continue to occur in the future. Yours, ———.

VIII.
INFANT BAPTISM.

"The entrance of thy words giveth light; it giveth understanding unto the simple."—PSALMIST.

MY DEAR BROTHER :—I have read very many prosy volumes, written in defense of infant baptism, in search of some legitimate argument in support of the practice. I have not found it. Special pleading I have found, and not a few sophisms, many of them too transparent to deceive any one, and others artful and quite plausible, yet really "baseless as the visions of the night." If there is a defense of infant baptism rising to the dignity of a solid, forcible argument, I have not met with it. Confessedly there is no "Thus saith the Lord" enjoining it, nor one single example in the Word of God to give it sanction. And yet many great denominations of Protestants, who claim to be Bible Christians, persistently continue the practice of it. They say, "The Bible is our only and sufficient rule of faith and practice in all matters of doctrine and of duty;" "The Bible is the religion of Protestantism;" but at the same time they cling to a Romish practice, which has no warrant in the Scriptures.

This is a fatal inconsistency in a vital matter. You may retort that no man is perfect; that the very best people are inconsistent in many things; and that those who are themselves confessedly somewhat imperfect ought to be lenient toward the imperfections of their friends; or you may remind me that every denomination has its own peculiar traditions and usages; and you may intimate very broadly that if other people do not like the usages of this or that church, it is their privilege to let it alone; and that you have the same right to baptize babes that I have to refuse to baptize them; though I have too high an opinion of your intelligence and good sense to suppose that you will think of urging considerations so indefensible. But the fact remains that some do press just such empty excuses for an unscriptural practice. As a matter of civil right—right guaranteed by the laws of the land—your right to sprinkle babes is exactly as great, and as secure, as my right to refuse to sprinkle them. And all true Baptists rejoice in that religious liberty which their Baptist fathers were so largely instrumental in securing, and which, as Baptists, we will be among the last to impair, surrender or destroy.

But though, in our opposite practices in respect to infant baptism, we have an equal *civil* right, yet morally, we can not both be equally right. If infant baptism is a scriptural ordinance, then I am doing a great wrong in discrediting it and in refusing to practice it. But, on the other hand, if it be not a scriptural practice, all pedobaptists are doing at least an equal wrong in adhering to it. I have no moral right to refuse to do anything that the Scriptures plainly enjoin, and you have just as little right to do, *in the name of the Lord*, anything that he has not authorized you to do. And that which is true of men individually, in this matter, is equally true of churches and of denominations. No church or denomination has the slightest right to adopt or retain any religious ordinance whatever, as a matter of tradition, or as an inheritance from the Fathers. Whatever the Divine Word requires, that, and that only, may they rightfully do; and if, in any church or denomination, any unscriptural usage exists, it is the immediate duty of that people to desist from it. The fair presumption is, that our Lord is wiser than men, than even the best and the wisest of men; and that it is the plain, simple duty of all his disciples not to mend or change his precepts and ordinances, but carefully and religiously to observe and obey them. And if any section of the great body of professed disciples of Christ do otherwise, and do so intentionally and persistently, then it justly becomes a matter of legitimate concern to all the rest of the great company of the redeemed. And since we are not to "suffer sin upon our brother," those who are aware of the wrong-doing are bound to protest against it, and to exhort those who are engaged in it to desist. For the Christian pilgrimage is not a sort of "happy-go-lucky" picnic, in which each man is a law to himself; nor is it a "go-as-you-please" tramp, but a well-defined race, in which every one, who strives for the crown, must conform to the regulations prescribed by the Master. And a genuine obedience is of more value in his sight, than any number of "usages" or "ceremonies" invented by men, though they may be very beautiful and pathetic, and though they were contrived, and have been perpetuated, with the most laudable motives. Indeed, he declares that "to obey is better than sacrifice," even when that sacrifice is legitimate.

Nor can the absence of such obedience be excused, in this case, on the plea of human imperfection; for it is not the result of any lack of ability. Certainly, those who practice infant baptism could refrain from it if they would. It is not a matter of infirmity, but of deliberate choice. They do it without scriptural warrant, just because they want to do it; or because it is the custom of their church; or because it is fashionable; or because, failing to do it, they would be subjected to criticism; or because of some fancied good that may come of doing it.

A case, illustrating this last class of motives for infant baptism, occurred some years ago, in an Eastern State. I repeat it as it was related to me by a friend—a man of unquestioned worth and piety.

An honest, industrious German farmer went to his neighbor, an aged Baptist minister, and asked permission to use his spring-wagon for a trip to town next day. The minister instantly granted his request; and then, knowing that his German friend was noted as a "keeper-at-home," he ventured to inquire the nature of his errand to the city.

"Vell, den," was the reply, "I goes dere shoost to haf dem dwins papdized, so dey vont pe so gross. Dey shoost gries unt gries all der dime, unt mine vife, she vos dired oud mit der grossness. Ven der briest papdize dem, dey vill pe no more so pad."

"Why, my friend," said the minister, "baptizing them will not stop their crying. They will be just as cross after they are baptized as they are now. You are quite welcome to the use of my wagon, but you are foolish to go so far on such an errand. You would be wiser to stay at home and attend to your work. Baptism will not do your twins any good whatever."

"Vell," said the German, "das is vot you dinks aboud im, unt you haf alvays peen mine vrent, unt von goot und kint napor; pud der papdism vas shoost so pedder as der tochter's bills vor dem gross dwins, unt I dry im."

So the next day he took the twins to town, and the priest, with all due gravity, sprinkled them. He returned home, in the confident assurance that, as he told his Baptist neighbor, when he returned the wagon: "Dem dwins don't nefer got so gross some more dill dey got pig."

Take two more illustrations of the same motives: A few months ago, a well-dressed lady, a resident of this city, called upon me, bringing with her a very feeble-looking babe, about two months old. She gravely and earnestly requested me to baptize it, saying that it had "decay of the flesh," and that the "old man" told her he could not cure it, as medicine would not take effect upon it until it had been baptized. I tried very earnestly, but apparently with very poor success, to show her the folly of supposing that baptism would have any effect upon the medicine, or the disease; or that it could, in any way, promote the cure of the babe. And I also endeavored to convince her that infant baptism is neither scriptural nor beneficial; but she "went away sorrowful," and in search of a more compliant minister. The result of her search I have never learned.

Subsequently, another lady called at my residence on a similar errand. Her babe, as she informed my daughter, for I was absent, had the "*go-backs*," whatever that may be, and she wanted it baptized, so that medicine would take effect.

My friend, Rev. Mr. S——, an able pedobaptist minister, to whom I related these circumstances, told me that such superstitious notions of baptism are quite common among a certain class of our German people. He did not seem at all surprised at my experiences in the matter, but seemed to regard it as a very common affair— a thing to be expected as a matter of course. He said they often called upon him to baptize their babes, so that medicine would take effect upon them. But he assured me that he had never complied with such requests. I honor him for his refusal to minister to such superstitions, and yet I must confess that, in my own opinion, baptizing children for the "go-backs" has in it the merit of a definite purpose. It proposes an end, and a very desirable one, the cure of a dangerous malady, and those who make such use of it, might, with much propriety, urge in defense of their action, the same reason recently urged by a political partisan in this region in favor of the election of the candidate of his party to the Legislature of the State, viz.: "He is not good for anything else, and surely he ought to be a good legislator." "Infant baptism," they might well exclaim, "infant baptism is not good for anything else, and certainly it ought to put a stop to the go-backs." And I am not sure that this notion is so much more superstitious than the entire practice of infant baptism, for that practice originated, not in the word of God, but in exaggerated and superstitious ideas of baptism, which was supposed to possess some sort of magical power, as I will presently prove by the testimony of many eminent and unimpeachable pedobaptist witnesses. It arose, not in Palestine, in the days of Christ or of his apostles, but in the churches of Alexandria and of North Africa, long after the apostles had ceased from their labors, and had entered into their refreshment and reward in the better land. And its origin and final establishment were due, not to any apostolic precept or example, but to the heretical and deadly notion that baptism is indispensable to the salvation of each human soul, and that without it no human being can be saved.

I have already presented to you a mass of evidence, proving by pedobaptist witnesses that infant baptism and sprinkling are not of the Bible. The article of Rev. J. Jacobi on "Baptism," from which I quoted in my letter on the "*Testimony of the Encyclopedias*," assures us that "infant baptism was established neither by Christ nor by his apostles." And in this statement he is supported by his friend, the great Neander, and by a host of the most competent pedobaptist writers. In these letters I propose to prove conclusively that infant baptism is not an apostolic institution, and I will produce pedobaptist witnesses of the highest character, witnesses that no man can impeach, to show its origin in the gross darkness and heresy that regarded baptism as a charm, and applied it to unconscious babes, that thereby they might be permitted to enter heaven. Some people sneer at the Baptists, and say, "There are no babes in the Baptist Churches." But Baptists do not think baptism essential to salvation; they regard it not as a saving ordinance, but only as a confessing ordinance, and, therefore, they do not apply it to infants, who are saved without it, and who are not fitted to make the solemn and responsible confession inseparable from it.

ERASMUS—"It is nowhere expressed in the apostolic writings that they baptized children."

DR. KNAPP—"There is no decisive example of infant baptism in the Scriptures."

BISHOP BURNET—"There is no express precept or rule given in the New Testament for the baptism of infants."

Is it not strange that the New Testament should be silent respecting a gospel ordinance? Is it not incredible?

CURCELLÆUS—"The custom of baptizing infants did not begin before the third age after Christ was born. In the former ages no trace of it appears. . . It was introduced without the command of Christ, and, therefore, this rite (infant baptism) is observed by us as an ancient custom, *but not as an apostolical tradition.*"

OLSHAUSEN—"There is altogether wanting any conclusive proof-passage for the baptism of children, in the age of the apostles, nor can any necessity for it be deduced from the nature of baptism."

Dr. Leonard Woods—*Infant Baptism.*—"Whatever may have been the precepts of Christ, or of his apostles, to those who enjoyed their personal instructions, it is plain that there is no *express precept* respecting infant baptism in our sacred writings. The proof, then, that infant baptism is a divine institution must be made out in another way. . . . I can by no means admit, as I intimated in a previous lecture, that the New Testament does not contain anything which fairly implies infant baptism. Still, it is evident that infant baptism is not introduced as a subject of *particular discussion* in the New Testament; that it is neither explicitly enjoined nor prohibited, and that neither the practice of baptizing children, nor the absence of such a practice is expressly mentioned." (Pages 11 and 105).

Georg Eduard Steitz, D. D.—Schaff-Herzog Ency.—*Art. Bapt.*—"There is no trace of infant baptism in the New Testament. All attempts to deduce it from the words of institution, or from such passages as 1 Cor. i. 16, must be given up as arbitrary. Indeed, 1 Cor. vii. 14, 'For the unbelieving husband is sanctified in the wife, and the unbelieving wife is sanctified in the husband; else were your children unclean, but now are they holy,' *rules out decisively all such deductions;* for, if pedobaptism were taught by Paul, he would have linked the salvation of the children with their baptism, and not with the faith of their parents. . . . Sponsors were probably unknown before the existence of infant baptism; with them also came in a special liturgy. . . . In the early Church preparation preceded baptism. . . . . *Tertullian, De Bapt.*, Chap. XX., says: 'They who are about to enter baptism ought to pray. . . . With the confession of all bygone sins.' . . . Great emphasis was early laid upon baptism. It was the condition of salvation—it gave pardon of sin, and imparted righteousness. . . . However correct may have been the views of the leaders of the Church, it is certain that the church-members entertained very erroneous notions. They ascribed to baptism a *magical efficacy*, and particularly the cleansing from sin, entirely irrespective of the religious state of the recipient; indeed, from the beginning of the fourth century the sad custom too widely prevailed of postponing baptism as long as possible, even to the death-hour, so that the recipient might continue his lax life, and *by this one act get rid of all the past sins, and enter heaven perfectly pure.* . . . . Baptism was considered indispensable to salvation. . . . Infant baptism came in quite naturally as the consequent of the belief in the necessity of baptism."

REV. A. T. BLEDSOE, D.D., LL.D.—"It is an article of our faith (Methodist Episcopal), that the baptism of young children (infants) is in any wise to be retained in the Church, *as most agreeable to the institution of Christ.* But yet, with all our searching, we have been unable to find in the New Testament a single express declaration or word in favor of infant baptism. We justify the right, therefore, *solely on the ground of logical inference*, and not on any express word of Christ or his apostles. This may, perhaps, be deemed, by some of our readers, a strange position for a pedobaptist. It is by no means, however, a singular opinion. *Hundreds of learned pedobaptists have come to the same conclusion*, especially since the New Testament has been subjected to a closer, more conscientious, and more candid exegesis than was formerly practiced by controversialists. In Knapp's Theology, for example, it is said: 'There is no decisive example of this practice in the New Testament; for it may be objected against those passages where the baptism of the whole families is mentioned, viz., Acts x, 42–48; xvi. 15–33, 1 Cor. i. 16, that it is doubtful whether there were any children in those families, and if there were, whether they were then baptized. From the passage Matt. xxviii. 19, it does not necessarily follow that Christ commanded infant baptism the *Matheteusate* is neither for nor against); nor does this follow any more from John iii. 5, and Mark x. 14–16. There is, therefore, no express command for infant baptism found in the New Testament, as Morus (p. 215, ¶ 12) justly concedes,' (Vol. 2, p. 524). Dr. Jacob also says: 'However reasonably we may be convinced that we find in the

Christian Scriptures the fundamental idea from which infant baptism was afterward developed, and by which it may now be justified, *it ought to be distinctly acknowledged that it is not an apostolic ordinance.*' In like manner, or to the same effect, Neander says: 'Originally, baptism was administered to adults; nor is the general spread of infant baptism, at a later period, any proof to the contrary; for even after infant baptism had been set forth as an apostolic institution, its introduction into the general practice of the church was but slow. Had it rested on apostolic authority, there would have been a difficulty in explaining its late approval, and that, even in the third century, it was opposed by at least one eminent Father of the Church' (p. 229).

"We quote this passage, not because its logic does, in every respect, carry conviction to our mind, but simply to show how completely *Neander concedes the point, that infant baptism is not an apostolic ordinance.* We might, if necessary, adduce the admission of many other profoundly learned pedobaptists that *their doctrine is not found in the New Testament, either in express terms, or by implication, from any portion of its language.*"—*Southern Review*, Vol. 14.

This testimony, from one of the most eminent of American Methodists, was quoted by Dr. Graves, in his debate with that champion of pedobaptism, Dr. Ditzler, of the Methodist Episcopal Church (South), and the correctness of the quotation was not questioned or denied. I take it from the report of that debate, published with the knowledge and concurrence of Dr. Ditzler. It is explicit and conclusive. Whatever else infant baptism may, or may not be, it is neither an *apostolic* nor a *New Testament* ordinance, in the judgment of *hundreds of learned pedobaptists.*

Now, permit me to place before you the testimony of an earnest Lutheran writer, an expositor whose praise is in all the ends of Christendom, a man whom his fellow-expositors delight to honor as *"the prince of exegetes:"*

H. A. W. MEYER, Th.D., on Acts xvi. 15.—"Of what members her family (Lydia's) consisted can not be determined. This passage and verse 33, with xviii. 8, and 1 Cor. i. 16, are appealed to in order to prove infant baptism in the apostolic age, or at least to make it probable. . . But on this question the following remarks are to be made:

"1. If, in the Jewish and Gentile families, which were converted to Christ, there were children, their baptism is to be assumed in *those* cases when they were so far advanced that *they could and did confess their faith on Jesus* as the Messiah; *for this was the universal, absolutely necessary qualification for the reception of baptism.*

"2. If, on the other hand, there were children still incapable of confessing, baptism could not be administered to those to whom that which was the necessary presupposition of baptism for Christian sanctification was still wanting.

"3. Such young children, whose parents were Christians, rather fell under the point of view of 1 Cor. vii. 14, according to which, in conformity with the view of the apostolic church, the children of Christians were no longer regarded as *akathartoi* (unclean), but as *hagioi* (holy), and that not on the footing of having received the character of holiness by baptism, but as having part in the Christian *hagiotes* by their fellowship with their Christian parents. . . . Besides, the circumcision of children must have been retained for a considerable time among the Jewish Christians, according to xxi. 21. Therefore,

"4. *The baptism of the children of Christians, of which no trace is found in the New Testament, is not to be held as an apostolic ordinance*, as, indeed, it encountered early and long resistance; but it is an *institution of the church*, which gradually arose in post-apostolic times, in connection with the development of ecclesiastical life and of doctrinal teaching, not certainly attested before Tertullian, and by him still decidedly opposed; and, although already defended by Cyprian, only becoming general after the time of Augustine, in virtue of that connection. Yet, even apart from the ecclesiastical premiss of a stern doctrine of original sin, and of the devil, going beyond Scripture, from which even exorcism arose, the continued *maintenance* of infant baptism, as the objective attribution of spiritually creative grace in virtue of the plan of salvation established for every individual in the fellowship of the church, is so much the more justified, as this objective *attribution* takes place with a view to the *future subjective appropriation.* And this subjective appropriation has so necessarily to emerge with the development of self-consciousness and of knowledge through faith, that in default thereof the church would have to recognize in the baptized no true members, but only *membra mortua* (dead members). This relation of connection with creative grace, in so far as the church is its sphere of operation, is a theme which, in presence of the attacks of Baptists and Rationalists, must overstep the domain of exegesis, and be worked out in that of dogmatics, yet without the addition of confirmation as any sort of supplement to baptism."

In other words, infant baptism, not being in the word of God, can not be established by the exposition of that Word, but must be defended by dogmatic assertions of some occult theory of salvation by virtue of one's relation to the church. But this defense, lame and unscriptural as it is, is not entitled to urge "confirmation as any sort of supplement to baptism." That is pretty good. Our author frankly confesses that, if the baptized infant should fail, in after years, to appropriate creative grace, the church must recognize in him only a *dead member.* Then it follows that the baptized infant is, by its baptism, *made a dead member of the church* to begin with. Is it not possible that the formalism and general godlessness of all State Churches is due to this fact? I commend the problem to you as one of grave import,—one that challenges the attention of every honest pedobaptist. But do not fail to note the statement of this "prince of exegetes," that there is *not a trace* of infant baptism in the New Testament, and extract from it just as much comfort as you can.

REV. WM. ORMISTON, D.D., LL.D., the American editor of the edition of Meyer, from which I quote says, in a note on this passage:

"This verse (15th) has often been quoted as evidence that infant baptism was the practice of the apostolic age. Commentators are divided in opinion on the force of the evidence afforded. *The passage, in itself, can not be adduced either for or against infant baptism.* It *might* be a presumption in favor of it. The practice itself rests on firmer ground than a precarious induction from a few ambiguous passages. *Plumptre:* 'The subject, however, does not properly fall under the domain of exegesis, but must be, as Meyer says, worked out in that of dogmatics.'"

There, that is a handsome and dignified way of backing down. Oh, the practice is not in the Scriptures—not a trace of it in the New Testament—but it rests on firm grounds, yes, on much "firmer grounds than a precarious induction from a few ambiguous passages." Poor, dear brethren, they boast and run—boast as they run—and cover an ignominious defeat with loud bragging about a change of base. That shows pluck, grand pluck—courage worthy a better cause, heroic, but—not apostolic. I like not to follow such leaders in a warfare and a retreat so utterly unscriptural.

So much is said by certain pedobaptist writers about 1 Cor. vii. 14, as a warrant for baptizing infants, that I desire to lay before you an exposition of that passage by that eminent Presbyterian divine, the late Albert Barnes. I transcribe it from his Notes on the place.

"*Else were your children unclean (akatharta)*. Impure, the opposite of what is meant by holy. Here observe (1), that this is a reason why the parents, one of whom was a Christian and the other not, should not be separated; and (2) the reason is founded on the fact that, *if* they were separated, the offspring of such a union must be regarded as illegitimate or unholy; and (3) it *must* be improper to separate in such a way, and for such a reason, because even *they* did not believe, and could not believe, that their children were defiled and polluted, and subject to the shame and disgrace attending illegitimate children. . . . This passage has often been interpreted, and is often adduced, to prove that children are 'federally holy,' and that they are entitled to the privilege of baptism on the ground of the faith of one of the parents. But against this interpretation there are insuperable objections: (1) The phrase 'federally holy' is unintelligible, and conveys no idea to the great mass of men. It occurs nowhere in the Scriptures, and what can be meant by it? (2) It does not accord with the scope and design of the argument. *There is not one word about baptism here: not one allusion to it; nor does the argument in the remotest degree bear upon it.* The question was not whether children should be baptized, but it was whether there should be a separation between man and wife, where the one was a Christian and the other not. Paul states that, *if such* a separation should take place, it would *imply* that the marriage was improper; and *of course* the children must be regarded as unclean.

"But how would the supposition that they were federally holy, and the proper subjects of baptism, bear on this? Would it not be equally true that it was proper to baptize the children whether the parents were separated or not? Is it not a doctrine among pedobaptists everywhere, that the children are entitled to baptism on the faith of *either* of the parents, and that

that doctrine is not affected by the question here agitated by Paul? Whether it was proper for them to live together or not, was it not equally true that the child of *a* believing parent was to be baptized? But (3) the supposition that this means that the children would be regarded as *illegitimate*, if such a separation should take place, is one that accords with the whole scope and design of the argument. 'When one party is a Christian and the other not, shall there be a separation?' This was the question. 'No', says Paul; 'if there *be* such a separation, it must be because the marriage is *improper;* because it would be wrong to live together in such circumstances.'

"What would follow from this? Why, that all the children that have been born since the one party became a Christian must be regarded as having been born while a connection existed that was improper, and unchristian, and unlawful, and, of course, they must be regarded as illegitimate. 'But,' he says, 'you do not believe this yourselves. It follows, therefore, that the connection, even according to your own view, is proper.' (4) This accords with the meaning of the word *unclean* (*akatharta*). It properly denotes that which is impure, defiled, idolatrous; unclean (*a*) in a Levitical sense (Lev. v. 2), (*b*) in a moral sense (Acts x. 28, 2 Cor. vi. 17, and Eph. v. 5). The word will appropriately express the sense of illegitimacy; and the argument, I think, evidently requires this. It may be summed up in a few words: 'Your separation would be a proclamation to all, that you regard the *marriage* as invalid and improper. From this, it would follow that the offspring of such a marriage would be illegitimate. But *you* are not prepared to admit this; you do not believe it. Your children you esteem to be legitimate, and they are so. The marriage tie, therefore, should be regarded as binding, and separation unnecessary and improper.' . . . . . 'I believe infant baptism to be proper and right, and an inestimable privilege to parents and to children. But a good cause should not be made to rest on feeble supports, nor on a forced and unnatural interpretation of Scripture. And such I regard the usual interpretation placed on this passage.'"

Now, my dear brother, what have you to offer against these learned pedobaptist witnesses? Can you refute their testimony? *Hundreds of them, men of profound learning, tell us that infant baptism is not taught in the New Testament, either directly or by implication.* They solemnly assure us that it is not an apostolic institution, that it rose in an age subsequent to that of the apostles, that it spread very slowly at first, and that it did not become the general practice of the churches until ages after the death of the apostles. Can you prove such testimony false? If you can not, then why persist in the unscriptural practice? *Is it not safer to be apostolic in your ways?* Yours, ———.

IX.

HISTORY OF INFANT BAPTISM.

"If the light that is in thee be darkness, how great is that darkness!"—JESUS.

MY DEAR BROTHER:—I am quite willing to rest the argument against infant baptism *on the simple, unvarnished history of its origin*, written and published by the greatest among pedobaptist historians of the Church, Dr. AUGUSTUS NEANDER. As you may not have his great work at hand, I will transcribe his account of the origin of infant baptism, or, rather, so much of it as will place the whole matter fairly before you. I quote from his Church History. He says:

"Baptism, at first, was administered *only to adults*, as men were accustomed to conceive baptism and faith as strictly connected. There does not appear to be any reason for deriving infant baptism from an apostolical institution; and the recognition of it, which followed somewhat later, as an apostolic tradition, serves to confirm this hypothesis. *Irenæus* [in second century—*Ed.*] is the first Father of the Church in whom we find any allusion to infant baptism; and in his mode of expressing himself on the subject, he implies at the same time its connection with the essence of the Christian consciousness, and testifies to the profound Christian idea out of which infant baptism arose, and which finally procured its universal recognition.

"*Irenæus* wishes to show that Christ did not disturb the development of that human nature which was to be sanctified by him, but sanctified it in all the several stages of its natural course. He came to redeem all by himself; all who, through him, are born again unto God —infants, little children, boys, young men and old. Therefore he passed through every age: for the infants he became an infant, sanctifying the infants; among the little children he became a little child, to sanctify those who are of this age, and at the same time to present to them an example of piety, uprightness and obedience; among the young men he became a young man, that he might set them an example and sanctify them to the Lord.

"It is here especially important to observe that infants (infantes) are expressly distinguished from children (parvulis,) and that Christ could *also* benefit them by his example; and that they are represented as capable of receiving from Christ, who had also lived through their period of life, simply an objective sanctification. This sanctification is imparted to them, in so far as they are born again to God through Christ.

"Now, in the mind of *Irenæus*, regeneration and baptism are intimately connected; and it is difficult to conceive how the term, 'being born again,' can be employed with respect to this age, to denote anything else than baptism. Infant baptism, then, appears here (in the opinion of *Irenæus*) to be the medium through which the principle of sanctification, imparted by Christ to human nature from its earliest development, became appropriated to children. The very idea of infant baptism implies that Christ, through the divine life which he imparted to and revealed in human nature, sanctified that nature from its earliest germ. The child born in a Christian family was to have this advantage; that he did not first come to Christianity out of heathenism, or the natural life of sin, but that, from the first dawning of consciousness, he should grow up under the imperceptible, preventing influences of a sanctifying, ennobling Christianity; that, in short, from the earliest dawn of the natural consciousness, a divine principle of life, capable of transforming nature, should be brought nigh to him, by which the divine portion might be attracted and strengthened before the ungodly principle could come into full activity, so that the latter might at once find here more than a counterpoise. In such a case, the new birth was not to constitute a new crisis, beginning at some definable moment, but it was to commence imperceptibly, and so to continue through the whole life. Baptism, therefore, the visible sign of regeneration, was to be given to the child at the very outset; the child was to be consecrated to the Redeemer from the beginning of its life. From the predominance of this idea, founded on the inmost essence of Christianity, *in the feelings of Christians*, resulted the practice of infant baptism.

"But immediately after *Irenæus*, in the last years of the second century, Tertullian appears as a zealous opponent of infant baptism; a proof that the practice was not universally regarded as an apostolical institution; for otherwise Tertullian would hardly have ventured to express himself so strongly against it. We perceive from his argument against infant baptism, that its advocates were already accustomed to appeal to Matt. xix. 14: 'Our Lord rejected not the little children, but commanded them to be brought to him that he might bless them.' Tertullian advises that, in consideration of the great importance of this rite, and *of the preparation necessary to be made for it on the part of the recipients*, men generally should rather delay baptism than hasten to it unprepared; and he takes occasion here to declare his particular objection to haste in the baptism of children. In answer to the argument for it, drawn from Christ's words, he replies: 'Let them come while they are growing up; let them come while they are learning, while they are being taught to what they are coming; but let them be made Christians when they are able to know Christ. What hurries the age of innocence to the forgiveness of sins? We show more prudence in the management of our worldly concerns; we trust the divine treasure to those who can not be entrusted with earthly property. Let them first learn to feel their need of salvation; so it may appear that we have given to those that wanted.'

"Tertullian evidently means that children should be led to Christ by instructing them in Christianity; but that they should not receive baptism until, after having been sufficiently instructed, they are led, from personal conviction, and by their own free choice, to seek for it with sincere longing of the heart. It may be said, indeed, that he is only speaking of the course to be generally followed; whenever there was momentary danger of death, baptism might be administered, even according to his views. But if he had thought this to be so necessary, it does not seem likely that he would have failed expressly to mention it. It would appear, in fact, from the principles laid down by him, that he did not believe that *any efficacy whatever* resided in baptism, unaccompanied by conscious participation and individual faith of the person baptized; nor could he see any danger accruing to the age of innocence from delaying it; a conclusion, however, by no means logically consistent with his own system.

"But when, on the one hand, the doctrine of the hereditary corruption and guilt of human nature, the consequence of the first transgression, was reduced to a more precise and systematic form; and when, on the other, from the want of a due distinction between the outward sign and the inward grace of baptism (the baptism by water and the baptism by the Spirit), the error became more and more firmly established that, without external baptism, no one soever could be delivered from that inherent guilt, could be saved from the everlasting punishment that threatened him, or be raised to eternal life; *and when the notion of the magical effects of the mere administration of the sacraments gained ground continually*, the theory was finally evolved of the *unconditional necessity of infant baptism.* About the middle of the third century this theory was already generally admitted in the North African Church.

"The Alexandrian Church, also, notwithstanding that in its theological and dogmatic character it was essentially different from the Church of North Africa, is found holding, even at a still earlier period, the doctrine of the necessity of infant baptism. Origen, in whose system infant baptism naturally finds its place, though not in the same connection of thought as it held in the system of the North African Church, declares it to be an apostolical tradition; an expression, by the way, which, perhaps, can not be regarded as of much weight, being made in an age when a strong inclination prevailed to derive from the apostles every ordinance which was considered of special importance; and when, moreover, so many walls had already been thrown up between it and the apostolic age, hindering the freedom of prospect.

"But if the necessity of infant baptism was acknowledged in theory, it was far from being uniformly recognized in practice. And, indeed, it was not always from the purest motives that men were induced to put off their baptism. The very same false notion of baptism as an *opus operatum*, which had led some to consider the baptism of infants as unconditionally necessary, led many others, who, indeed, mistook the nature of this rite in a far grosser and more dangerous degree, to delay their baptism to the hour of death, in order that, freely abandoning themselves in the meantime to their lusts, they might yet be cleansed by the magical annihilation of their sins, and so pass, without hindrance, into eternal life. We have already noticed the pious indignation and energy with which Tertullian, who, in other respects, was opposed to haste in baptism, combated this error. It seems probable, also, that infant baptism furnished the *first* occasion for the appointment of sponsors, or god-parents; for, as in this case, the persons baptized *could not themselves make the necessary confession of faith and renunciation*, it became necessary for others to do it in their name; and these, at the same time, engaged to take care that the children should be rightly instructed in Christianity, and trained up in a life corresponding to the baptismal vow. They were, therefore, called sponsors (sponsores). Tertullian alleges it as an argument against infant baptism, that the sponsors assumed an obligation which they might be prevented from fulfilling, either by their own death or by the untoward conduct of the child.

"And, first, as it respects *baptism*. It may be remarked that infant baptism—as we have observed that the fact was already toward the close of the preceding period—was now (A. D. 312 to 590) generally recognized as an apostolical institution; but from the theory on this point we can draw no inference with regard to the practice. It was still very far from being the case, especially in the Greek Church, that infant baptism, although acknowledged to be necessary, was generally introduced into practice. Partly the same mistaken notions which arose from confounding the thing represented by baptism with the outward rite, and which afterward led to the over-valuation of infant baptism, and, partly the frivolous tone of thinking, the indifference to all higher concerns, which characterized so many who had only exchanged the pagan for a Christian outside;—all this together contributed to bring it about that, among the Christians of the East, infant baptism, though in theory acknowledged to be necessary, yet entered so rarely, and with so much difficulty, into the church life during the first half of this period.

"Accustomed to confound regeneration and

baptism, believing that they were bound to connect the grace of baptism with the outward ordinance, with the performance of the external act; failing to perceive that it should be something going along with, and operating through the entire life, many pious, but mistaken, parents, dreaded entrusting the baptismal grace to the weak, unstable age of their children, which grace, once lost by sin, could never be regained. They wished rather to reserve it against the more decided and mature age of manhood, as a refuge from the temptations and storms of an uncertain life. To a mother who acted on this principle, says Gregory of Nazianzen: 'Let sin gain no advantage in thy child; let it be sanctified from the swaddling clothes, consecrated to the Holy Ghost. You fear for the divine seal, because of the weakness of nature. What a feeble, faint-hearted mother must you be! Anna consecrated her Samuel to God even before he was born; immediately after his birth she made him a priest, and she trained him up in the priestly vesture. Instead of fearing the frailty of man, she trusted in God!' Others, unlike this mother, were induced, not by an error of the understanding, but by a delusion springing from an altogether ungodly temper, to defer their baptism to a future time. They had formed their conception of God, of whom they would gladly have been relieved from the necessity of thinking, only as an Almighty Judge, whose avenging arm appeared to their unappeased conscience ready to strike them; and they sought in baptism a means of evading the stroke, without being willing, however, to renounce their sinful pleasures. They were disposed to enter into a sort of compact or bargain with God and Christ, to be permitted to enjoy, as long as possible, their sinful pleasures, and yet, in the end, by the ordinance of baptism, which like a charm, was to wipe away their sins, to be purified from all their stains, and attain to blessedness in a moment. Hence, many put off baptism until they were reminded by mortal sickness, or some other sudden danger, of approaching death. Hence it was, that in times of public calamity, in earthquakes, in the dangers of war, multitudes hurried to baptism, and the number of the existing clergy scarcely sufficed for the wants of all.

"In the case of many who first received baptism in the later period of life, this proceeding was no doubt attended with one advantage— *that the true import of the baptismal rite might then be more truly expressed.* It was not until after they had been led, by some dispensation affecting the outward or inner life, to resolve on becoming Christians with the whole soul, that they applied for baptism. And the ordinance, in this case, was not a mere *opus operatum,* but really constituted to them the commencement of a new era of life, truly consecrated, in the temper of the heart, to God. Thus it was, that many made it a point, from the time of their baptism, to enter upon the literal observance of Christ's precepts; they would no longer take an oath, and not a few outwardly renounced the world and became monks, which, at all events shows what importance they attached to this ordinance. But, on the other hand, the cause of delaying baptism, with numbers, was their want of any true interest in religion, their being bred and living along in a medley of pagan and Christian superstition; nor can it be denied that the neglect of infant baptism contributed to prolong this sad state of things. By means of baptism, children would have been immediately introduced into a certain connection with the church, and at least brought more directly under its influences, instead of being exposed, as they now were from their birth, to pagan superstition, and often kept at a distance, in their first training, from all contact with Christianity. To commend their children to God and to the Savior in prayer, was not the custom of parents; but rather to call in old women, who were supposed to possess the power of protecting the life of infants by amulets and other devices of heathen superstition.

"As it respects the doctrine concerning baptism, from which, for reasons stated under the preceding period, the doctrine of regeneration was not severed, we must observe that the difference here again became strongly marked, which we discern in the views of the Eastern compared with those of the Western Church, with regard to human nature and the doctrine of redemption, namely: that in the Western Church, with original sin, the negative effect of the redemption in procuring deliverance from this, and in the Eastern Church, on the other hand, the positive effect of the redemption, considered in the light of a new creation, were made especially prominent. Thus Gregory of Nazianzen calls baptism a more divine, exalted creation than the original formation of nature. Thus, too, Cyril of Jerusalem, addressing the candidate for baptism, says: 'If thou believest, thou not only obtainest the forgiveness of sins, but thou effectest also that which is above man. Thou obtainest as much of grace as thou canst hold.' This difference would be strongly marked, especially in the case of infant baptism. According to the North-African scheme of doctrine, which taught that all men were, from their birth, in consequence of the guilt and sin transmitted from Adam, subjected to the same condemnation, that they bore within them the principle of all sin, deliverance from original sin and inherited guilt would be made particularly prominent in the case of infant baptism as in the case of the baptism of adults. And this was favored by the ancient formula of baptism, *which, however, originated in a period when infant baptism had, as yet, no existence, and had been afterward applied, without alteration, to children,* because men shrank from undertaking to introduce any change in the consecrated formula established by apostolical authority, though Christians were by no means agreed as to the sense in which they applied this formula. 'Accordingly,' says Gregory of Nazianzen, 'to the children baptism is a seal (a means of securing human nature *in the germ* against all moral evil by the higher principle of life communicated to it); for adults it is, moreover, forgiveness of sin and restoration of the image degraded and lost by transgression!' Hence, he looks upon infant baptism as a consecration to the priestly dignity, which is imparted to the child from the beginning, that so evil may gain no advantage over him. In a homily addressed to the neophites, Chrysostom specifies ten different effects of grace wrought in baptism; and then he complains of those who make the grace of baptism consist simply in the forgiveness of sin. True, the difference here becomes manifest between the more rhetorical Chrysostom and the systematic Augustine; for the latter would have referred those ten specifications to one fundamental conception, in which they might all be summed up together. But, at the basis of this difference, lay that other, which has already been noticed in respect to the general mode of Christian intuition. Hence Chrysostom adds: 'It is for this reason we baptize also infants, though they are not, like others, stained with sin, that so holiness, justification, adoption, heirship and brothership with Christ may be imparted to them through Christ, that so they may be members of Christ.'

"These words of Chrysostom are, indeed, known to us only in the Latin translation, and through a citation of the Pelagian writer Julian. But their genuineness is evinced by the fact that Augustine had nothing to object to them on that score, but must seek to deprive Pelagianism of this support by giving the passage another interpretation. And, in truth, this passage strictly accords with the peculiar character already noticed, belonging to the type of doctrine, not only of the Oriental Church generally, but of Chrysostom in particular.

"Julian is wrong in explaining the words of Chrysostom wholly according to his own sense, as if Chrysostom had meant to say that human nature is still born in the same state as it was at first; for this is, in fact, at variance with his doctrine concerning the innocence lost by the sin of the first man. But if Julian was wrong in this single respect, that he contemplated the words wholly out of their connection with Chrysostom's entire mode of thinking on doctrinal matters, Augustine, on the other hand, manifestly tortured them, when he explained them according to *his* system, as referring barely to the absence of actual personal sin; for in this case the antithesis made by Chrysostom would, in fact, not hold good.

"Isidore, of Pelusium, also replies to the question why infants, who are without sin, should be baptized, in the following way: Some, who took too narrow a view of the matter, said it was that they might be cleansed from the sin transmitted to them from Adam. This, indeed, he said, was not to be denied, but it was not the only reason. This would still be a thing not so great after all; but there would be besides many other gracious gifts communicated to them, which far exceed any possible attainments of human nature. Infants were not only delivered from the punishment of sin, but, moreover, had imparted to them a divine regeneration, adoption, justification, fellowship with Christ. The remedy amounted to far more than the mere removal of an evil.

"Theodore, of Mopsuestia, seized in this case upon only one side, or moment, of the Oriental Church doctrine, which moment, in infant baptism, was ever made the more prominent one; but the other he dropped entirely, as his system required that he should. It is, according to his doctrine, the same state of human nature, mutable and liable to temptation, in which the first man was created, and in which all infants are born. Baptism, in the case of adults, has a twofold purpose: to bestow on them the forgiveness of sin, and to exalt them, by fellowship with Christ, to a participation in his freedom from sin, and his moral immutability, which is the passing over from the first portion of the development of life in humanity, into the second, which is fully entered upon only at the general restoration. That which is received at baptism is the principle and pledge of that freedom from sin which will then first come to be fully realized. In the case of infant baptism, then, the forgiveness of sin, according to Theodore's doctrine, does not properly come into consideration; but its purpose and object is simply the imparting of that new and higher life, exempt from sin, of which the entire human nature stands in need. He distinguishes, accordingly, a twofold meaning of the forgiveness of sin, to the bestowment of which the formula of baptism refers. He supposed, therefore, in this latter respect, the same supernatural communication in the case of infant baptism, as in the case of the baptism of adults; though, following out the natural bent of his acute and discriminating understanding, he carefully distinguished here, too, that which is merely the symbol and vehicle, from that which is the working principle, lest that should be ascribed to the magical operation of the water, which could only be ascribed to the agency of the Holy Spirit. The water, he maintained, according to the comparison employed by Christ in his conversation with Nicodemus, stood related to the creative power of God, in the new and higher birth, as the body of the mother to the creative power of God in the natural birth.

"This mode of apprehension was adopted, as we learn particularly from the explanations of Cœlestius and of Julian, by the Pelagians; though it did not, in their system, rest upon the same foundation as in the Oriental and in the Antiochian systems. In this way we must understand what Cœlestius says in the creed which he sent to Rome: 'Infants must, according to the rule of the Universal Church, and according to the declaration of the Gospel, be baptized in order to the forgiveness of sin. Since our Lord has determined that the kingdom of heaven can be bestowed only on the baptized, and since the powers of Nature are not adequate to this, it must be the free gift of grace. It is clear that Cœlestius, in denying that any sinfulness adhered to infants, could understand baptism for the forgiveness of sins, in this case, only after the same manner with Theodore, of Mopsuestia; and, accordingly, he understood also, in like manner with the latter, by the kingdom of heaven, that which transcends the limits of human nature; that which can only be bestowed upon it by a higher communication from God. Thus the Pelagian, Julian, though he absolutely denied the possibility of any forgiveness of sins in the case of infants, could still declare that baptism, having been once instituted by Christ, must be acknowledged as universally valid, and necessary for every age; *that eternal condemnation awaited every one who denied that this rite was profitable also for children.* 'The grace of baptism,' said he, 'is everywhere the same; but its effects appear different, according to the different relations and circumstances of the subjects of it. In some the negative effect, the forgiveness of sin, must precede the positive, the exaltation of man's nature. In infants, the effect is only to *ennoble* the nature, which remains in its original condition of goodness.' Although it would be natural for the Pelagians, according to the principles of their system, to ascribe to baptism, as being an external act, a merely symbolical import, yet they did not find it possible to disentangle themselves wholly from the church tradition of their period; but they sought to reconcile what they found in that tradition, as best they could, with their own principles, which had arisen in an entirely different way. Moreover, with regard to the relations of the divine matter to the external sign, of regeneration to outward baptism, they had precisely the same notions which were the prevailing ones in the Church; for this becomes sufficiently clear from what they taught respecting the effects of infant baptism; and Julian expressed himself on this point with distinctness and precision.

"On the other hand, the doctrine which, ever since the time of Cyprian, by the habit of confounding the inward grace with the outward sign in baptism, had become predominant, especially in the North African Church, *the doctrine of the damnation of unbaptized infants* appeared to the Pelagians as something revolting, something whereby a tyrannical, arbitrary will was imputed to the Divine Being. But, on the other hand, they must themselves, however, according to the theory just unfolded, suppose the higher grace of participating in the highest stage of blessedness in the kingdom of heaven was conditioned solely on the obtaining of baptism; and even *they* found this asserted in the words of Christ to Nicodemus, as even *they* made no distinction of the baptism of the

Spirit from the baptism with water. Accordingly, they must, of necessity, affirm, with regard to unbaptized infants, that, although free and exempt from punishment, they were still excluded from that higher state of being, and attained only to a certain intermediate state. This was what Cœlestius really meant to say in the declarations above cited.

"And to the same result, on this subject, must every one have been led, who was inclined to adopt the Oriental mode of considering the effects of baptism, and would consistently follow out the matter to a definite conclusion; unless he supposed a universal redemption or restoration, as the final end, to which that intermediate state was destined to prove a point of transition for unbaptized infants. Such an intermediate state Gregory of Nazianzen also assigned for those who were unbaptized through no fault of their own. Augustine himself had once entertained a like opinion. Ambrose, of Milan, believed, also, that it was necessary to infer from the words of Christ to Nicodemus, that none could enter the kingdom of heaven without baptism; but it was his opinion, though he had no confidence in it, that unbaptized infants would be exempted from punishment. Pelagius himself shrank from expressing any decided opinion on this point, though, by logical thinking, it was absolutely out of his power to avoid that consequence of his principles. He affirmed of unbaptized children that of one thing he was sure, namely, that they could not, as innocent beings, suffer punishment consistently with the divine justice; but what would become of them was more than he knew, doubtless because he was of the opinion that no distinct declaration on this point could be found in the Sacred Scriptures.

"But then Augustine could, however not without good reason, accuse the Pelagians of inconsistency, when they charged the advocates of the doctrine of absolute predestination with imputing arbitrary will to God, while they themselves were still more involved in this error, by supposing that God excluded innocent beings from the kingdom of heaven, which he bestowed on others who were in no respect more worthy of it. The notion, moreover, of an intermediate place between the state of woe and the kingdom of heaven was a thing altogether unscriptural, and incredible in itself; for man, being in the image of God, was destined to find his bliss in communion with God, and out of that communion could be no other wise than wretched. The Council of Carthage, A. D. 418, finally condemned, in its XI. Canon, the doctrine of such an intermediate state for unbaptized children, on the ground that nothing could be conceived as existing between the kingdom of God and perdition; but then, too, according to the doctrine of this Council, the eternal perdition of all unbaptized infants was expressly affirmed—a consistency of error revolting to the natural sentiments of humanity. It is worthy of notice, however, that this particular passage of the Canon is wanting in a portion of the manuscripts.

"But such being the prevailing doctrine concerning baptism, reflecting minds must now have been struck with the difficulty of conceiving how a divine influence could take effect in the case of infants devoid of all conscious moral action of their own. Augustine, by means of his correct principles, above explained, respecting the essence of sacraments, might have found out a better way if he had not been fettered by the authority of the church doctrine. His reply, indeed, explains nothing; but it proceeds from a profound feeling of the essential nature of Christian fellowship. He says: 'The faith of the church, which consecrates infants to God, in the spirit of love, takes the place of their own faith; and albeit they possess, as yet, no faith of their own, yet there is nothing in their thoughts to hinder the divine efficacy.' His scheme, then, amounted to this: that as the child, in its corporeal and independent existence, was fully developed, was supported by the vital forces of Nature in its bodily mother; so ere it came to the independent development of its spiritual being in its consciousness, it is supported by the heightened vital forces of that spiritual mother, the church—an idea which would involve some truth, supposing the visible church corresponded to its ideal, when applied, without being so literally understood, to infant baptism."

Now, my dear brother, tell me, if you can,

how it is possible for me to resume the practice of infant baptism in the face of this tremendous mass of unimpeachable pedobaptist testimony against it. Your very best exegetes being judges, the New Testament is entirely silent respecting it. Your most learned and able historians agree that it is an invention of men, gotten up since the age of the apostles. Your greatest church historian shows that it is the child of one of the most corrupt and deadly of all heresies. He traces its rise and progress, as it developed out of the notion of sacramental salvation. Each stage of its growth is clearly shown. Baptism first came to be looked upon as a rite of magic power, by which men could be saved, no matter how vile—and without which even the sweet, guileless babe must be forever lost. Then was infant baptism born of heresy and superstition, nurtured by priestcraft and perpetuated by ecclesiastical power, reinforced by the sword of the State.

Christ and his apostles were not pedobaptists; they were Baptists, your ablest writers being judges. All the Romish Popes are pedobaptists. Indeed, by *that craft* they gained and retain their power. This is a plain, undeniable historic fact. Infant baptism is the mother of the Papacy. Here is the real pedigree of the great apostasy. Baptismal regeneration, born of ignorance, brought forth infant baptism, of which were born the *State Church*, Romanism, and the *Church-above-the-State*, Popery. Without infant baptism the Papacy could never have been. Without it, one generation would end the Roman Catholic hierarchy. *No infant baptism, no Pope.* That is as plain as that two and two are four. And the hierarchy appreciates that fact, and the Council of Trent pronounced a curse upon all who reject infant baptism or speak against it. Why, then, should I, in this matter, quit the company of Christ and his apostles and go over to the company of the Pope? Why, in this matter, should you be on the side of the Pope rather than on the side of Christ?

Infant baptism, as your own witnesses prove, is not scriptural; it was not instituted by Christ or his apostles. Then, why cling to it so tenaciously? What good does it do? Are those who are baptized in infancy any better than those who are not? Who will dare assert that they are? Recently I heard a venerable pedobaptist divine, Rev. Dr. B——, declare, in a public address, that when he supplied the pulpit of a very prominent Episcopal Church, in one of our great cities, a few years ago, the children were not in the sanctuary, but at home, on the streets, or in the saloons. And that was on the Lord's day, and those children were the "baptized children of the church," of which we hear so much. *Of what value was their infant baptism?*

You know perfectly well that it is of no practical utility. It can no more suffice to save the soul than to render efficacious medicines intended to heal the body. Were I to charge you with believing there is any saving virtue in it, you would repel the charge vigorously and indignantly. And yet you persist in your practice of it, just as if it were an apostolic and sacred ordinance. But, as your own ablest brethren demonstrate, it is neither apostolic nor scriptural; and, as the facts of daily observation abundantly prove, it has no saving, transforming power over character. I wonder you do not abandon it. What is it but the weakness and menace of Protestantism—the grappling-iron of that awful ecclesiastical despotism, Romanism? I tell you most solemnly, my dear brother, there is nothing good in it—absolutely nothing; but the evils that flow from it are legion, and the greatest of them—next to the dishonor it casts upon the authority of Christ in his own house—is the superstition it fosters among the people. Practically, multitudes come to regard it as a cure for the *"go-backs"* of the body and of the soul. To them, it is indeed a charm, under the protection of which they feel safe. Insensibly, but really, they put it in the place of Christ; make it their trust; regard it as their ticket of admission into heaven, and rest contentedly in their sins, deluded by a false hope. And the evil does not end there. They take their places in the churches—duly christened, but strangers to Christ; and the inevitable result is, a Christless church, or, at the best, a church in which the Christless element predominates. And a church made up very largely of baptized sons of Belial can always be counted on as a perpetual fountain of darkness and death. The history of Lutheranism in Germany is an illustration in point. Why is it that evangelical pedobaptists are to-day sending missionaries to Germany? Simply because infant baptism has neutralized the great Reformation. "If the light that is in thee be darkness, how great is that darkness." Yours, ———.

X.

MORE WITNESSES.

"Thy word is a lamp unto my feet, and a light unto my path."—PSALMIST.

MY DEAR BROTHER:—I do not wonder that you are astonished at the great number and the high character of the witnesses whom I have cited from your own ranks against the practice of sprinkling, and against infant baptism. But there are many more of the same sort, and their numbers are daily increasing. And they testify against their own practices with an amazing directness and unanimity. That they should do so, and still adhere to those practices, which, by their own showing, are unscriptural, is a difficult problem; one that concerns all good people, but especially all good pedobaptists.

The explanation may, perhaps, be found in the influence of habit and environment holding them with a fearful grip in the practice of things once believed to be apostolic, but now known to be inventions of men. It is no easy matter to break away from long-established habits and usages, and especially in matters ecclesiastical and of wide-spread public notoriety. It involves a most humiliating confession of error; challenges the criticism and hostility of brethren who are less enlightened; rends asunder old associations full of tender and sacred memories, destroying friendships that otherwise would terminate only with life itself; in a word, it jeopardizes reputation, position, influence and personal comfort, in a thousand ways, demanding tremendous and almost immeasurable sacrifices, and, to me, it is no wonder that many good men shrink from an ordeal so severe. Of course, I am speaking of men in public life—ministers, pastors, teachers and expositors—men whose opinions, practices and changes are matters of public interest. These men are, to a large extent, tied up by their environment. In accepting their positions and work, they have given themselves, as hostages, into the keeping of their brethren, to abide in the old ways. They did it honestly, and in all good faith, in early life, not anticipating any need of any change of usages. Then, by and by, came new knowledge, and as the light increased they were confronted by facts very stern and unpleasant.

And it may be that many good men, in the presence of an ordeal so crucial, find it far easier to take refuge in the convenient plea of indifferency—so common in the ranks of our pedobaptist friends—than boldly to risk all for the truth of Christ. Or, making a merit of necessity, as many other good people have done, *they may have put a confession of the truth in the place of the practice of it,* just as certain other wrong-doers think it enough to say frankly, "Oh, yes, I know I am doing wrong; I do not deny that; I freely confess it," and then keep right along doing the same wrong things, as if the confession of the wrong could make the doing of it right.

But be the solution of this problem what it may, the fact is undeniable, that an ever-growing "cloud of witnesses," men of the highest rank of scholarship and piety, testify clearly and fully against their own pedobaptist practices as altogether unscriptural. Indeed, it is getting to be a thing so common, that many good people are in real danger of coming to regard it as a mere matter of course, and so to attach to such testimonies far less importance than justly belongs to them.

Suppose, for a single moment, if you can, that some eminent Baptist were found testifying that immersion was unknown in the apostolic age, or that infant baptism was the universal practice of those times, what an amazing sensation it would produce. It would be a new thing under the sun, and there would be a mighty stampede of Baptists. Or, imagine an eminent Baptist translator writing, "I, indeed, baptize (sprinkle) you with water." It would create a moral earthquake in the Baptist camp. But here are large numbers of pedobaptists—an increasing number of them every year—bearing testimony just as fatal in its character to pedobaptist practices. That it is not equally fatal in its effect on those practices, is a fact not to be denied, and a fact, it must be conceded, not very much to the credit of our pedobaptist friends.

When eminent pedobaptist writers translate *baptizo* by *immerse*, as some of them actually do, it is time to ask gravely: "Why is it that they do not conform their practice to the command of our Lord as translated by themselves?" Indeed, this question is already an old one, and the answer has long been stereotyped. Rome says the Church has power to change the ordinances at her pleasure. Calvin treats the form of the ordinance as a matter of indifference, even when that form is definitely determined by the divine command, as in the rite of baptism. And in this one thing, if nothing else, the great mass of our pedobaptist friends are loyal Calvinists. But in this I praise them not, deeming it far better that men should be loyal to Him who says, "Ye are my friends if you do whatsoever I command you." Just how a man can go about the task of convincing our Lord that he is his friend, while refusing to obey his precepts, is more than I can understand. Of one thing I am very sure; it is a very bold, hazardous thing to do. Jesus himself condemns it in advance, in those pregnant words: "He that loveth me not, keepeth not my sayings." (John xiv. 24.)

But, leaving this matter to each one's conscience, I will now place before you the testimonies of a few more representative pedobaptist writers:

JOHN CALVIN.—*Institutes, Book IV., Chap.* 15, *Sec.* 19.—"The word baptize signifies to immerse, and it is certain that immersion was the practice of the ancient church."

MARTIN LUTHER.—"First, the name baptism is Greek. In Latin it can be rendered immersion, as when we immerse anything into water, that it may be all covered with water. And, although that custom has now grown out of use with most persons (nor do they wholly submerge children, but only pour on a little water), yet they ought to be entirely immersed and immediately drawn out, for this the etymology of the name seems to demand."

MELANCTHON.—"Baptism is an entire act; to-wit, a dipping."

CASAUBON.—"The manner of baptizing was to plunge or dip them into the water, even as the word baptism plainly shows."

ARCHBISHOP SECKER.—"Burying, as it were, the person baptized in water and raising him out again, without question was anciently the more usual method."

LEIGH.—"The native and proper signification of it is to dip into water, or to plunge under water."

GODET.—*On Luke.*—"The rite of baptism, which consisted in the plunging of the body more or less completely into the water, was not in use at this time" [*i. e.*, when John the Baptist began his ministry].

H. A. W. MEYER, D.D.—*On Matt. iii.* 11.—"*En* is, in accordance with the meaning of *baptizo, immerse* (*eintauchen*), not to be understood *instrumentally*, but on the contrary, as *in*, in the sense of the element wherein the immersion (*eintauchen*) takes place."

PROF. CHARLES ANTHON, LL.D.—"The primary meaning of the word (*baptizo*) is to dip, or to immerse; and its secondary meanings—if it ever had any—all refer in some way or other to the same leading idea. . . . *Sprinkling* and *pouring are entirely out of the question*" [*i. e.*, as definitions of *baptizo*].

SAMUEL CLARK, D.D.—"In the primitive times, the manner of baptizing was by immersion, or dipping the whole body into water."

VITRINGA.—"The act of baptizing is the immersion of believers in water. This expresses the force of the word."

GROTIUS.—"That baptism used to be performed by immersion, and not by pouring, appears from the proper signification of the word, and by the places chosen for the administration of this rite."

MEDE.—"There was no such thing as sprinkling used in the apostles' days, nor for many days after them."

WITSIUS.—"It can not be denied that the native signification of the word *baptein* or *baptizein*, is to plunge or dip."

VOSSIUS.—"To *baptize* signifies to plunge."

WILSON.—"To baptize—to dip one into water, to plunge one into water."

POOLE.—"A great part of those who went out to hear John were baptized; that is, dipped in the Jordan."

WETSTEIN.—"To baptize is to plunge, to dip. The body, or part of the body, being under water is said to be baptized."

SAURIN.—"The ceremony of wholly immersing us in water when we were baptized, signifies that we died to sin."

MALDONATUS.—"For in Greek to be baptized is the same as to be submerged."

BISHOP TAYLOR.—*On Matt. iii.* 16.—"The custom of the ancient-churches was not *sprinkling*, but *immersion;* in pursuance of the sense of the word in the commandment, and the example of our blessed Savior."

STORR AND FLATT.—*Biblical Theology, Art. Baptism.*—"The disciples of our Lord could understand his command in no other way than as enjoining *immersion;* for the baptism of John, to which Jesus himself submitted, and also the earlier baptism of the disciples of Jesus, was performed by *dipping* the subject into cold water.

"And that they actually did understand it so, is proved; partly by those passages of the New Testament, which evidently allude to immersion, . . . and partly from the fact that immersion was so customary in the Ancient Church, that even in the third century the baptism of the sick, who were merely sprinkled with water, was entirely neglected by some, and by others was thought inferior to the baptism of those who were in health, and who received baptism not merely by aspersion, but who actually bathed themselves in water. This is evident from Cyprian (Epistle 69., ed. Bremae, p. 185, etc.,) and Eusebius (Hist. Eccles., L. vi., cap. 43), where we find the following extract from the letter of the Roman Bishop Cornelius: 'Novatus received baptism on the sick-bed by aspersion (*perichutheis*), if it can be said that such a person received baptism.' No person who had, during sickness, been baptized by aspersion, was admitted into the clerical office.

Moreover, the old custom of immersion was also retained a long time in the Western Church —at least in the case of those who were not indisposed. And even after aspersion had been fully introduced in a part of the Western Churches, there yet remained several who, for some time, adhered to the ancient custom. Under these circumstances it is certainly to be lamented that Luther was not able to accomplish his wish with regard to the introduction of immersion in baptism, as he had done in the restoration of wine in the eucharist."

Now, my brother, weigh carefully the statements of these last witnesses—Storr and Flatt. They admit all that Baptists claim with respect to the facts. They frankly tell us that *Christ prescribed immersion;* that his apostles could understand his command in no other manner than as enjoining immersion; that immersion was the custom of the Ancient Church, and that this custom was retained a long time in the Western Churches. They assure us that the change from immersion to sprinkling ought never to have been made, and that Luther desired to restore the old practice of immersion, but did not succeed in doing so. Now, if these witnesses tell the truth, then it follows beyond question—

1. That immersion was established by command of Christ.

2. That it was set aside in defiance of his command.

3. That the practice of sprinkling is against his authority.

4. That it is simply *custom* against *Christ.*

5. That in this controversy the Baptists are right.

6. That in adhering to immersion, they are loyal to Christ.

7. That in insisting upon immersion as baptism, they honor and obey Christ.

Here are seven good and conclusive reasons why every Baptist should remain a Baptist, and why all other true disciples of the Master should hasten to become Baptists as soon as possible.

BISHOP DAVENANT.—"In the Ancient Church they did not merely sprinkle, but immersed those whom they baptized."

REV. GEORGE CAMPBELL, D.D.—"The word *baptism*, both in sacred authors and classical, signifies to dip, to plunge, to immerse, and was thus rendered by Tertullian, the oldest of the Latin Fathers." "It is always thus construed suitably to this meaning." "It is never, in any case, sacred or profane, employed in the sense of rain or sprinkle."

PROF. MOSES STUART.—"Both these words (*bapto* and *baptizo*) mean to dip, to immerse, to plunge into anything liquid. All lexicographers and critics of any note are agreed in this."

ROSENMULLER.—"To baptize is to immerse or dip; the body, or the part of the body which is to be baptized, going under the water."

SCHOLZ.—"Baptism consists in the immersion of the whole body in water."

DR. DÖLLINGER.—"The fact that the Baptists are so numerous, or even the most numerous of all religious parties in North America, deserves all attention. They would, indeed, be yet more numerous, were not baptism, as well as the Lord's Supper, as to their sacramental significance, regarded in the Calvinistic world as something so subordinate, that the inquiry after the original form appears to many as something indifferent, about which one need not much trouble himself. The Baptists are, however, in fact, from the Protestant standpoint, unassailable; since for their demand of baptism by submersion, they have the clear Bible text, and the authority of the church, and of her testimony, is regarded by neither party."

DR. TOWERSON.—*On Baptism.*—"As touching the outward and visible sign of baptism, there is no doubt it is the element of water, as is evident from the significance of the word baptism, which signifies an immersion, or dipping into some liquid thing."

DR. FRITZSCHE.—*On Rom. vi. 4.*—"We are therefore (*i. e.*, because, when we were baptized by immersion into water, Christ's death was presented before us *in an image of burial*) as was Christ, *deposited in a tomb by baptism, that we might be declared dead.*"

Dr. Porson.—"The Baptists have the advantage of us. *Baptizo* signifies a total immersion."

Bishop Browne.—*Smith's Bible Dictionary, Art. Baptism.*—"The language of the New Testament and of the primitive Fathers, sufficiently points to immersion as the common mode of baptism. John the Baptist baptized in the river Jordan (Matt. iii.); Jesus is represented as coming up out of the water after his baptism (Mark i. 10). Again, John is said to have baptized in Enon, because there was much water there" (John iii. 23).

Archbishop Sumner.—*Lectures.*—"John was baptizing, *i. e.*, immersing in water, those who came to him for this purpose, confessing their sins."

Dr. Stier.—*Words, Vol. VIII., p. 306.*—"The perfect immersion is not accidental in form, but manifestly intended in *baptizein eis.*"

Selden.—*Works, Vol. VI., Col.* 2008.—"In England, of late years, I ever thought the person baptized his own fingers, rather than the child."

Buddeus.—*Theol. Dogm. Vol. I., C. 1., Sec. 5.*—"The words BAPTIZEIN and *baptismos* are not to be interpreted of aspersion, but always of immersion."

Bucanus.—*Inst. Theol.*—"*Baptism*, that is, immersion, dipping, and by consequence, washing. *Baptistery*, a vat, or large vessel of wood or stone, in which we are immersed, for the sake of washing. *Baptist*, one that immerses or dips."

HOSPINIAN.—*Hist. Sacr., Book* II., *C.* I, *p.* 30.
—"Christ commanded us to be baptized, by which word it is certain immersion is signified."

BEZA.—*On Matt. iii.* 13.—"But *baptizo* signifies to dip, since it came from *bapto*, and since things to be dyed are immersed. Christ commanded us to be baptized, by which word it is certain immersion is signified. Neither does the word *baptizo* signify to wash, except by consequence, for it properly signifies to *plunge into*, for the sake of tinging or dyeing."

RICHARD BAXTER.—*On Matt. iii.* 6.—"We grant that baptism then (in apostolic times) was by washing the whole body." ... . "In our baptism, we are dipped under the water, as signifying our covenant profession, that, as He was buried for sin, so we are dead and buried to sin."

G. DIODATI.—"In baptism, being dipped in water, according to the ancient ceremony, it is a sacred sign unto us that sin ought to be drowned in us by God's Spirit."

LANGE.— *On Matt. iii.* 1, 6, 11.—"This baptism was administered by immersion, and not merely by sprinkling. It denoted purification, but not only washing, but submitting to sufferings akin to death. So far as is known, this rite was not accompanied by the usual sacrifices, but the deepest spiritual part of the sacrificial services—the confession of sins—preceded the immersion.

6. "And were baptized [immersed] in the

Jordan, confessing their sins. *Immersion was the usual mode of baptism* and the symbol of repentance. According to Meyer, repentance was symbolized by immersion, because every part of the body was purified. But, in that case, the whole body might have been washed without immersion. We must keep in view the idea of a symbolical descent into the grave, or the death of sin, although this view, as explained in Rom. vi., could not yet have been fully realized at the time. . . . A full confession of sins accompanied the act of immersion.

11. "I, indeed, baptize in [*en*] water (immersing you in the element of water) unto repentance. He shall baptize, or immerse, you in the Holy Ghost and in fire. He will either entirely immerse you in the Holy Ghost as penitents, or, if impenitent, he will overwhelm you with the fire of judgment (and at last with hell-fire).'"

PROF. L. L. PAINE, D.D.—"It may be honestly asked by some, Was immersion the primitive form of baptism? and if so, what then? As to the question of fact, *the testimony is ample and decisive.* No matter of church history is clearer. The evidence is all one way, and all church historians of any repute agree in accepting it. We can not claim even originality in teaching it in a Congregational seminary. And we really feel guilty of a kind of anachronism in writing an article to insist upon it. It is a point on which ancient, mediæval and modern historians alike—Catholic and Protestant, Lutheran and Calvinist—have no controversy. And the simple reason for this unanimity is, that the statements of the early Fathers are so clear, and the light shed upon these statements from the early customs of the church is so conclusive, that no historian who cares for his reputation would dare to deny it, and no historian who is worthy of the name would wish to."

DEAN STANLEY. — *"Essay on Baptism."* — "For the *first thirteen centuries* the almost universal practice of baptism was that of which we read in the New Testament, and *which is the very meaning of the word 'baptize'*—that those who were baptized were *plunged, submerged, immersed into the water.* That practice is still, as we have seen, continued in Eastern Churches. In the Western Church it still lingers amongst Roman Catholics in the solitary instance of the Cathedral of Milan, amongst Protestants in the austere sect of the Baptists. It lasted long into the middle ages. Even the Icelanders, who at first shrank from the waters of the freezing lakes, were reconciled when they found that they could use the warm water of the geysers. And the cold climate of Russia has not been found an obstacle to its continuance throughout that vast Empire. Even in the Church of England, it is still observed in theory. Elizabeth and Edward the Sixth were both immersed. . . . IT HAD, NO DOUBT, THE SANCTION OF THE APOSTLES AND OF THEIR MASTER. It had the sanction of the venerable churches of the early ages, and of the sacred countries of the East. Baptism by sprinkling was rejected by the whole ancient church (except in the rare case of death-beds, or extreme necessity) as no baptism at all. Almost the first exception was the heretic Novatian. It has still the sanction of the powerful religious community, which numbers amongst its members such noble characters as John Bunyan, Robert Hall and Havelock. . . . But, speaking generally, the Christian civilized world has decided against it. It is a striking example of the triumph of common sense and convenience over the bondage of form and custom. Perhaps no greater change has ever taken place in the outward form of a Christian ceremony with such general agreement. It is a greater change even than that which the Roman Catholic Church has made in administering the sacrament of the Lord's Supper in the bread without the wine. For that was a change which did not affect the thing that was signified; whereas, the *change from immersion to sprinkling has set aside the larger part of the apostolic language regarding baptism, and has altered the very meaning of the word.*

"But, whereas, the witholding of the cup produced the long and sanguinary war of Bohemia, and has been one of the standing grievances of the Protestants against the Roman Catholic Church, the withdrawal of the ancient rite of immersion, decided by the usage of the whole ancient church to be essential to the sacrament of baptism, has been, with the exception of the insurrection of the Anabaptists of Munster, adopted almost without a struggle. It shows the wisdom of not imposing the customs of other regions and other climates on those to whom they are not congenial. *It shows how the spirit which lives and moves in human society can override even the most sacred ordinances.* . . . Another change is not so complete, but is perhaps more important. In the apostolic age and in the three centuries which followed, it is evident that, as a general rule, those who came to baptism came in full age, of their own deliberate choice. We find a few cases of the baptism of children; in the third century we find one case of the baptism of infants. Even amongst Christian households, the instances of Chrysostom, Gregory Nazianzen, Basil, Ephrem of Edessa, Augustine and Ambrose are decisive proofs that it was not only not obligatory, but not usual. *They had Christian parents, and yet they were not baptized till they reached maturity.* The liturgical service of baptism was framed entirely for full-grown converts, and is, only by considerable adaptation, applied to the case of infants. Gradually, however, the practice spread, and after the fifth century the whole Christian world, East and West, Catholic and Protestant, Episcopal and Presbyterian (with the single exception of the sect of Baptists before mentioned), have baptized children in their infancy. Whereas, in the early ages, adult baptism was the rule, and infant baptism the exception, in later times infant baptism is the rule, and adult baptism the exception.

"What is the justification of this almost universal departure from the primitive usage? There may have been many reasons, some bad, some good. One, no doubt, was the *superstitious feeling already mentioned, which regarded baptism as a charm, indispensable to salvation,* and which insisted on imparting it to every human being who could be touched with water, however unconscious. Hence the eagerness with which the Roman Catholic missionaries, like St. Francis Xavier, have made it the chief glory of their mission to have baptized heathen populations wholesale, in utter disregard of the primitive or Protestant practice of previous preparation. Hence the capture of children for baptism without the consent of their parents, as in the celebrated case of the Jewish boy Mortara. Hence the curious decision of the Sorbonne, quoted in *Tristram Shandy*. Hence, in the early centuries and still in the Eastern churches, coextensive with infant baptism, the practice of infant communion, both justified on the same grounds, and both based on the mechanical application of biblical texts to cases which, by their very nature, were not contemplated in the apostolic age."

But, my dear brother, I am puzzled not a little by the fact that there are those claiming to be men of God—teachers of the people, too— who, in the face of the overwhelming evidence, demonstrating beyond any reasonable doubt that sprinkling and infant baptism are neither scriptural nor apostolic, stand up and tell the people that they are scriptural and apostolic practices. What shall I say of these men? What am I to think of them? Would you have me become one of them? Are you fond of their company?   Yours, ———.

XI

PEDOBAPTIST DEFENSES.

"He that loveth me not, keepeth not my sayings."
—Jesus.

My Dear Brother.—While the concessions of pedobaptist writers are numerous and strong, their defenses are few and weak. Instead of taking refuge in the strong ramparts of the citadel of divine truth, they seek protection behind an ever-varying line of temporary breastworks, constructed of brush-like, perishable materials. One fortifies with some decayed fragments of the ancient Jewish circumcision; another creeps behind the old and tottering walls of an imaginary, old-time Jewish Church; while a third builds up a brave-looking stockade of the most approved guesses about certain possible babies in the households baptized by the apostles. Not a few dodge behind those late tables or couches in Mark vii. 4; while others construct a trelliswork of twisted Greek prepositions; and others, still, hide behind "The element applied to the subject," and profess to find, in the Pentecostal descent of the Holy Spirit, a literal baptism, justifying aspersion.

These, indeed, are only samples of their wonderful and ever-changing devices, whose name is legion. But there is still another class of defenses employed by our pedobaptist friends when their usual sophisms and assumptions prove inadequate. This consists of wholesale and persistent assertions. And sometimes they raise such a din, that many poor Baptists are frightened into a trembling silence; while many good people, mistaking assertion for argument, are cheated, by this Chinese mode of warfare, into a complete surrender.

Assumptions, sophisms, assertions—these three words fairly describe all the defenses of infant baptism and sprinkling. Take each several defense urged by Catholic or Protestant, subject it to a thorough, rigid analysis, and it will invariably prove to be either a mere assumption, a transparent sophism, or a bald, unwarranted assertion. Let us test this matter a little. The Catholic justifies the practice of his Church, in the baptism of infants and in the substitution of sprinkling for immersion, by the plea that the

"Church is above the written Word," and may, of right, change the precepts and ordinances of the gospel at her pleasure. What is this but an assumption of power altogether unwarrantable, and undeniably sacrilegious? All true Protestants will unite heartily in denouncing it as the very essence of Antichrist. Yet it is the only Catholic defense of pedobaptism.

But the Protestant pedobaptist, when called upon to defend his own pedobaptist practices, resorts at once to a series of assumptions, all of which are indefensible, and some of which are hardly less reprehensible than that which he so roundly condemns in the Catholic. He boldly assumes that obedience to the command of Christ, in the ordinance of baptism, is a matter of little or no importance; that, whether we do the thing enjoined by our Lord or something else that he did not enjoin, is a matter of indifferency; thus setting aside his will in deference to our own wish and preference. Thus, by his assumption, our Protestant pedobaptist friend claims for himself, individually, a power of setting aside the law of Christ, and of changing his ordinances, which he indignantly denies to the entire Catholic Church. In order to find some shadow of excuse for persisting in the unscriptural practice of infant baptism, some of our pedobaptist brethren assume the *identity* of the old Jewish Commonwealth and the Church of Christ—an assumption so baseless and so ridiculous, and involving such a host of absurdities, that it is difficult to realize that it can find lodgment, for a single moment, in a healthy mind.

Then the related assumption, that baptism is really circumcision in another form, is so preposterous and so plainly opposed to scriptural facts, and carries with it logical sequences so stupendous, that one hardly knows how to deal with a mind that can entertain it; and more especially since the use made of it, and the arbitrary limits assigned it, clearly demonstrate that those who urge it do not themselves believe it. For, if the assumption be granted, then it establishes not only infant baptism, but also the duty of baptizing *all* the children and *all* the servants in the family, no matter what their ages or their characters.

Others assume that there were babes in the households baptized by the apostles, and then, assuming that the apostles actually baptized those hypothetical babes, they gravely proceed to build up the doctrine of infant baptism on these and kindred assumptions equally baseless. And, to cap the climax of these brazen assumptions, with a cheek that is monumental, they assume that the burden of proof rests on those who refuse to accept their assumptions as historic facts, in the absence of any credible evidence. So the tricky Spiritualistic medium, taking you into a darkened room, contrives some mysterious raps, and then exclaims: "There, that's the spirits; and if it isn't the spirits, what is it?"—adroitly throwing the burden of proof upon the objector. If you are not very green and too utterly creduous, you will reply: "Well, prove that it's the spirits, and then I will believe it. You assert it, and the burden of proof rests upon you." Such common sense treatment has a very depressing effect upon the apostles of Spiritualism. It checks the growth of that wild delusion in a way most discouraging to its friends. And the same sensible method applied to infant baptism, would have a like effect upon that unscriptural practice. Let good people demand evidence instead of assumption, in its behalf, and it will soon become a thing of the past.

The literature of pedobaptism is peculiarly rich in sophisms. A few samples will illustrate the beauty and value of the entire assortment. Because true believers are said to be "children of Abraham" (Gal. iii. 7), we are gravely told that the *children of such believers* are also children of Abraham. *Spiritual regeneration* and *natural generation* are purposely confounded, treated as identical—a most transparent and unwarrantable sophism. The pretended argument is completely unmasked, the moment it is fully and formally stated, thus: "You are a child of Abraham by a *spiritual regeneration*, therefore your *unregenerate* child is also a child of Abraham by *natural generation*." A false translation of a Greek preposition is made the basis of a labored sophism in favor of sprinkling. In our common English Version we read, in Matt. iii. 11: "I, indeed, baptize you *with* water;" and our scholarly pedobaptist friends, who know perfectly well that the true reading is *in* water, ring the changes on *with* water, and gravely assure us that Inspiration teaches that *the element is applied to the subject*, and not the subject to the element, and that John the Baptist being judge, we are to be baptized *with* water, not *in* it. That the true reading is *in* water needs no further proof than is found in the list of readings preferred by the American Committee, Class No. IX., in Appendix to *Oxford Revision* of 1881. The American Committee, composed almost entirely of eminent pedobaptist scholars, unanimously preferred the reading *in water;* yet grave pedobaptist divines still urge the old, exploded sophism, as if it were a legitimate argument.

The baptism of the Spirit on the day of Pentecost is made the basis of a similar sophism. "I will tell you," said a prominent Congregational minister, "why I left the Baptists and became a Congregationalist. The account of the baptism of the Spirit on the day of Pentecost convinces me that, while our Baptist brethren are right in holding that immersion is baptism, they are wrong in that they do not accept sprinkling also as baptism. On the day of Pentecost the Spirit was poured out upon the disciples, the element was applied to the subject, and Inspiration calls that baptism. And so, while I believe immersion is baptism, I regard sprinkling, also, as scriptural baptism." To this statement a friend made this reply: "My dear brother, you are in a dilemma. As a thinking man you must ultimately admit that your reason, just given, for quitting the Baptists and accepting sprinkling as scriptural baptism, is a first-class sophism, wholly destitute of truth, or you must reject Revelation altogether and avow yourself a materialistic atheist. As an intelligent and thoroughly honest man, there is no third course open to you. For your supposed argument assumes a literal pouring out of the Spirit, as water is poured out of a cup; it regards the *element* as a material substance literally applied to the subject. But if this—which is essential to your argument—be true, then the Holy Spirit is matter, a material substance; then *God is matter* and *matter is God*, and all religions are impossible and false, and materialistic atheism is true. But if the Holy Spirit be *not* a material substance, then he was not *actually* poured out, the element was not *actually* applied to the subject, and your argument is not *actually* an argument, but only a first-class sophism that proves nothing."

You know, my dear Bro. H———, that on the day of Pentecost the Holy Spirit was not literally poured out, nor sprinkled out, nor were the disciples literally immersed in him, but that they were filled and overwhelmed by his presence and his transforming influences; and that he is said to have been poured out, and his work is called a baptism, with reference, solely, to the overwhelming *effects* thereby produced, without the most distant allusion to the *method* of his coming or to the *mode* of his gracious and transforming operation. And you are also aware that the word *baptism*, in this Pentecostal, figurative use of it, derives all its force from the well-known overwhelming of the candidate, inseparable from a literal baptism, or immersion in water, so that this figurative use of the word amounts almost to a complete demonstration of its literal meaning.

Another favorite sophism with many of our pedobaptist friends is to ask, "How were the Isralites 'baptized unto Moses in the cloud and in the sea'?" (1 Cor. x. 2.) Here again the word is used figuratively, the cause being put for the effect. Those who are "baptized into Christ have put on Christ:" *i. e.*, they have by that act, in a public manner, professed themselves his disciples; they have fully committed themselves to him, as their Lord and their Redeemer, to lead them out of the bondage of sin and death into the heavenly Canaan. In precisely the same way those who followed Moses into the sea beneath the cloud, committed themselves entirely to him, as their trusted and chosen leader, to conduct them out of the prison-house of Egyptian bondage into the rest and the liberty of the earthly Canaan.

As the disciple, in his baptism, commits all to Christ, so they committed all to Moses, and with reference solely to this complete commitment to Moses, their act is called a baptism. It may be that in their treatment of this matter our pedobaptist brethren act in good faith, but if so, their conduct is hardly creditable to their intelligence.

But, fruitful as they are in assumptions and sophisms, our pedobaptist friends challenge admiration by the number and the boldness of their assertions. You can hardly imagine anything adverse to the practice of immersion that has not been roundly asserted by some fearless champion of sprinkling. Thus we have been told that John the Baptist could not have baptized by immersion, *since the river Jordan is not deep enough to immerse people in;* that the three thousand on the day of Pentecost could not have been immersed, *since there was not enough water in Jerusalem for the immersion of such a multitude;* and all this in the face of the undeniable facts that the Jordan is so deep as to be fordable in a very few places only, and that the public reservoirs of water in Jerusalem were numerous and very large, containing water enough for the immersion of hundreds of thousands of people. Thus, too, we are told that immersion is a barbarous, indecent sort of practice, suited only to a rude age of society, and that it is not practicable in cold climates, together with much more of the same sort.

And occasionally some very bold champion

of sprinkling, rises up to remark that "*immersion is nowhere commanded in the Scriptures.*" An instance of this capital sort of assertion occurred quite recently. The *Christian Observer* is a Presbyterian newspaper, published in Louisville, Ky. In its issue of January 16, 1884, on the first page, is a remarkable article, contributed by a certain D. D., resident somewhere in Virginia. From the caption of his article, "Church or Bible—Which?" one might infer that he is a very pious man—a truly good man—and greatly concerned because of the real or supposed encroachments of some ambitious church upon the authority of the Divine Word. The article proves that he is, indeed, a most peculiarly sensitive man in this respect, since he actually attempts to cudgel the Baptist Churches, as if they were guilty of usurping or attempting to usurp some sort of authority over the Word of God or the consciences of men —a people whose great mission has ever been to insist upon the absolute supremacy of the word of the Lord over all churches, and over all who profess themselves disciples of Christ.

And this is a sample of his style of assertion: "We are told that not merely baptism, but *one exclusive mode of baptism*, is essential for approaching the Lord's Table. But take the Bible, search it all through, and find one such teaching. It is not there. Don't misunderstand. *Our Lord did command baptism.*"

Dear, generous man, in this last sentence, which I have taken the liberty to put in italics, he concedes, nay, asserts, a fact of grave importance. Baptism rests on a very solid foundation — the command of our Lord — this pedobaptist writer being witness. In his next sentence he is thoroughly orthodox, and all Baptists will take pleasure in indorsing his italicized declaration that *"every one who professes to obey him should be a baptized person."* That, so far as it goes, is good, sound Bible doctrine, and equally sound Baptist doctrine, too. And the next four sentences of his article are also thoroughly orthodox, Baptists being the judges. I quote them: "'Ah!' says Close Communion, 'that is just the point. You must be immersed, or you are disobedient to Christ; therefore have no right to the Lord's Supper.' This means that Christ commanded *immersion*, or *dipping*, as the only baptism. The assertion is boldly made." Yes, and it is as true as it is bold, for it embodies the exact truth of God's Word on this matter. But hear our Presbyterian D.D. still further: "But take the Bible again, and search it through. Where is that command? It is not there. *Not one verse nor word in the Bible puts any one under the water.* This mode is unknown to the Bible. Christ never *once* commanded immersion. But a branch of the Church commands it, and *insists upon it as essential.* Which is greater? . . . Now, as there is no command for, nor example of, immersion, in the Bible, the demand for immersion, as a prerequisite for the Lord's Table, is without divine warrant. *It is based entirely upon the human views of a branch of the Church.* Is it, then, binding? Which is greater—the Church or the Bible?"

There is audacity for you. Such assertions leave nothing more to be asserted. They border on the sublime of a certain sort. Their author is certainly a brave man, brave to the verge of utter recklessness. He is not afraid of facts. If they are against him, so much the worse for the facts. He rushes against them without a tremor, and denies their existence with an amazing assurance.

Seriously, it is difficult to deal with such utterly unwarrantable assertions with forbearance. In charity toward their author, I presume he is a Christian, made such in his infancy by a beautiful christening; but really I am afraid his christening didn't take—failed to strike in, so to speak—and so left him with very imperfect ideas of the importance of truth-telling, as one of the Christian graces, whence it happens that he seems to make assertions with far more zeal than prudence and integrity.

What will he do with the immense mass of pedobaptist evidence against him already cited in these letters, especially the testimony of Prof. H. A. W. Meyer, the late Dean Stanley, Storr and Flatt and Dr. Langé, not to mention scores of others? And how will he go about it to translate *Baptizontes* in Matt. xxviii. 19, and *e Baptisthe hupo Ioannou eis ton Iordanen*, in Mark i. 9?

Any possible honest translation of *Baptizontes* will suffice to refute perfectly his high-sounding assertions, and to demonstrate the well-established fact that our Lord does actually command immersion, and that only such as are properly immersed are properly baptized. If any pedobaptist doubts this fact, let him test it by attempting or procuring such a translation, and he will speedily be convinced of its absolute truth.

The balance of the article from which I have been quoting is taken up with sophisms and crude assertions directed against our Baptist practice of restricted communion. It is the same old, stale hash to which we have been so long and so liberally treated. I will not bore you with quotations from it, for there is nothing in it worthy the attention of earnest, intelligent men.

But in the same paper, of January 9, 1884, there is an editorial on the fourth page, under the caption, "WHO MAY COMMUNE?"—an editorial so candid, so able and so conclusive that I gladly quote it entire. It is the production of a Presbyterian editor, and accords thoroughly with the principles and usage of the Presbyterian Church on the question discussed; and I present it to you as a complete and triumphant scriptural vindication of our Baptist usages in respect to the Lord's Supper, premising only that which you already know, that by baptism we understand the immersion of a professed believer in Christ. He says:

"A correspondent sends us the following question: 'One question I would be pleased to have answered in your paper, thus: If, during the hour of the sermon preceding the administration of the Lord's Supper, a person becomes enlightened and fully believes in the cleansing power of the blood of Christ, and is truly *converted*, would it be according to the teachings of the Scriptures and of our Church for him to partake of the Lord's Supper without or before there is an opportunity of joining the church or being baptized?'

"To us there seems to be little difficulty in the reply. *It is not in accordance with the Word of God for a man to partake of the Lord's Supper before he has made a public profession of his faith in Christ, or before he has been baptized.*

"The fact that this New Testament sacrament was instituted at the Passover Supper shows its substantial *identity of significance* with the Passover. As the Passover lamb represented the Messiah that *was to come*, the Lord's Supper represents the Messiah *that has come*. The law of the Passover was distinct, that no one could partake of the lamb till after he was circumcised. Whatever reason caused the enactment of that provision would prevail also in the case raised by our correspondent.

"The significance of the sacraments points to the same conclusion. Baptism signifies the entrance of the believer on a life of piety; the 'putting off of the sins of the flesh,' 'our ingrafting into Christ,' our claiming 'the benefits of the new covenant,' and our profession of faith in Christ. The Lord's Supper represents our feeding on Christ by faith. The one represents our admission to the feast; the other, our partaking of it. If a man should commune before baptism, he would be eating the feast before he entered the room; feeding on Christ before he even professed to be Christ's. *This would be nonsense.*

"In accordance with this is the example of

the apostles. We can not recall a case where a man was allowed to commune before baptism; *there are abundance of cases in which the man was baptized before communing; in fact, every recorded case follows this order.* This fact is the more significant because many of these Jewish converts had been circumcised and might claim that this was an equivalent for baptism. *Yet at Pentecost the apostles required a profession of faith, and baptism, even from circumcised Jews, before admission to the Lord's Supper.*

"The Presbyterian Church follows these instructions in inviting to the Lord's Table those who love the Lord Jesus in sincerity, *and have manifested their love by a public profession of faith, in some evangelical church.*

"The position is fortified by the necessities of the case. The apostle Paul bids the churches to 'let all things be done decently and in order.' How can the 'order' of the church be maintained, if each individual were to be allowed to decide for himself to what Christian privileges he is entitled? The very idea of church government implies that the converted sinner must apply to the regular authorities of the church for admission before he partakes of the sacrament peculiar to church-members alone."

Now, my brother, I commend to your prayerful consideration this Presbyterian defense of the old apostolic practice of restricted communion, so bitterly denounced by multitudes of pedobaptists when adopted and enforced by

Baptists. If it is true and scriptural for Presbyterians, why is it not equally so for Baptists? And if, as Baptists firmly believe, and as hosts of the wisest and most learned pedobaptists frankly confess, the immersion of a professed believer is the only scriptural baptism, how can Baptists honestly do otherwise than refuse to invite to the Lord's Table those who have not obeyed the Lord Jesus in scriptural baptism? If sprinkling is not the act that Christ enjoins as baptism, then all those who have been sprinkled instead of being immersed are, in fact, not baptized. Believers they may be, but they are not *baptized believers*, and therefore are not scripturally qualified to partake of the Lord's Supper, our Presbyterian brethren themselves being judges. Why, then, should Baptists be traduced and vilified incessantly for their fidelity to Christ and to the order of his house? Is it not enough that our pedobaptist friends set aside the authority of Christ in substituting rantism for baptism, and in rantizing infants, without adding unlimited abuse of such as are unwilling to sanction such disobedience?

Now suppose the editor, whose article I have just quoted, should become convinced that, after all, immersion is the only scriptural baptism, and that professed believers are the only scriptural subjects of baptism, what could he do but take his place with close communion Baptists? To-day the only legitimate question at issue between Baptists and Presbyterians, aside from the question of church government, is that of baptism—what it is and to whom it may be administered. Their views of doctrine generally, and *their avowed views of the principles regulating admission to the Lord's Table are identical.* Let the question of baptism be settled on its own merits by an appeal to the Word of God, honestly, faithfully and fully translated into our vernacular, and Baptists will cheerfully abide the consequences. Let assumptions, sophisms, assertions and abuse give place to the Word of God. On that Word Baptists are firmly planted. There they learn that John the Baptist immersed such, and such only, as professed penitence, saving only our Lord himself, whom he reluctantly immersed into the Jordan "to fulfill all righteousness." There they hear Jesus saying, "Go teach all nations, *immersing* [*Baptizontes*] them," etc. "He that believeth and is baptized [*Baptistheis*] shall be saved." There they see the words of Christ obeyed by his inspired apostles, who first preach the gospel, and then baptize such as believe, and such only. The word of the Lord is plain; its meaning unmistakable. Baptists can not do otherwise than obey it. Why is it that pedobaptists refuse to do likewise? My brother, I dare not return to you, but you can come to us, and *Christ will approve.* Will you do it?

Yours, ———.

XII.

THE FOOT-LIGHTS FOCALIZED.

"If ye know these things, happy are ye if ye do them."—JESUS.

MY DEAR BROTHER :—In this series of letters, I have placed before you a vast mass of evidence, drawn from the most approved pedobaptist sources, demonstrating the unscriptural origin of infant baptism and sprinkling. I have called these testimonies FOOT-LIGHTS, because they throw such a flood of light upon the scene. And it can not be denied that they make the situation interesting for our pedobaptist friends, exhibiting them as grave actors in a very solemn drama, contrived and foisted upon the churches by those ancient twin imposters—heresy and superstition.

The situation is certainly very awkward for those actors; but the illumination, "though for the present grievous," may bring forth "the peaceable fruits of righteousness," as it assuredly will in the case of each one who is rightly "exercised thereby." It is always unpleasant to be caught napping when one is reputed to be wide awake; and sometimes good people get cross about it and say foolish things; and it may be so with some of our pedobaptist friends when aroused by these penetrating FOOT-LIGHTS. But why should a Christian man repel the light, or persist in practices honestly but ignorantly adopted, when they are clearly seen to be unscriptural and wrong? It were "more noble" by far to face the music good-naturedly, and to "search the Scriptures daily" to see whether these things are true. And I doubt not that very many of our pedobaptist friends will act in this rational way, and, acting thus, they will be astonished at the correctness of these FOOT-LIGHTS, and confess their fidelity to the truth. Nor will they stop there; but, having learned the truth, as true disciples of the Master they will hasten to do it. And in that grand company of obedient ones I hope to see my dear old friend, whose deliverance from the meshes of atheism and conversion to Christ gave me such great joy long years ago.

These FOOT-LIGHTS are foot-lights in their offices only. In quality, brilliancy and power, each one of them is a vast concentrated headlight. Among the many scores of witnesses whose testimony I have placed before you in these letters, not one is "below par" in learning and credit. They are, each and all, men of the highest order of scholarship—men whose position and influence are thoroughly established. As witnesses in this controversy they are every way competent, and their testimony amounts to a demonstration that Baptists are in the right. Permit me, in this closing letter, to sum up their testimony—to focalize it, so to speak—that you may the more easily and clearly discern its completeness, and that you may feel somewhat its invincible force and yield your judgment to its convincing power.

1. *The lexicons teach that the Greek word for baptism means immersion, and that to baptize is to immerse.* The fact that they so teach is indisputable. One of the foremost among American pedobaptist scholars, Moses Stuart, assures us that "all lexicographers and critics of any note are agreed in this." This being true, it follows that *our Lord commanded immersion*, and that *only those who have been immersed* have obeyed that command. It also follows that *sprinkling is not baptism at all*, and therefore, that it is not scriptural baptism. From this it follows also that *those persons who have*

been sprinkled, instead of being immersed, *have not been baptized.* That the lexicons voice the judgment of the learned world, will not be disputed by men who are intelligent, candid and honest.

2. *The great mass of the encyclopedias confirm the testimony of the lexicons, and show that immersion was the ancient practice of all the churches, and that during many hundreds of years.* Some of them also show that infant baptism was not established by our Lord, nor by his apostles, and that it was unknown in the apostolic age, and for at least one hundred and fifty years afterward. Those of the encyclopedias that do not affirm the post-apostolic origin of infant baptism, do not deny it. *The encyclopedias are against infant baptism.*

3. *The great pedobaptist historians of the church testify unanimously that immersion was the old apostolic practice, and that it continued to be the general custom of Christendom for many ages.* They also testify that *infant baptism* is not of apostolic origin, but that it arose long after the apostolic age; and the greatest among all pedobaptist church historians, Neander, gives an elaborate account of the heresies and superstitions out of which it was gradually evolved. And he shows conclusively that infant baptism

was born of the heresy of baptismal regeneration, nursed and nourished by an almost incredible superstition, favored by dense and almost universal ignorance, and that even then it attained to general acceptance only through many ages of doubt, dissent and conflict.

It is undeniable that ecclesiastical history, as it is voiced by pedobaptist historians of the greatest eminence, is against infant baptism, demonstrating the historic fact that it is not an apostolic institution, but an invention of subsequent and very corrupt ages.

4. *A large number of most credible pedobaptist writers assure us that immersion continued to be the general practice of the Christian world for thirteen hundred years.* Not until the fourteenth century did sprinkling obtain official recognition as of equal validity with immersion, and then only in the Church of Rome. This fact is established in these letters by a large number of thoroughly competent pedobaptist witnesses.

5. *All pedobaptist expositors, excepting only two or three very modern ones, concede that in Rom. vi. 4, the apostle alludes to "the ancient baptism by immersion."* The array of witnesses on this point is overwhelming. Men of every pedobaptist denomination in Christendom, embracing a vast company of the most eminent

scholars and expositors, assure us that the inspired writer alludes to immersion; and in the whole Christian world there are found, in all the ages, only two or three who in any way dissent from this general verdict. But such apostolic allusion leaves no room to doubt that immersion was the apostolic baptism, and if so, it must have been the baptism commanded by our Lord, and substantially the same as that to which he himself submitted at the hands of John the Baptist in the waters of the Jordan. It is, then, beyond any reasonable doubt, the baptism which he to-day requires of his people, and at which so many who profess to be his disciples are so accustomed to sneer.

6. *Hosts of the ablest and most learned of pedobaptist scholars frankly admit that infant baptism is not taught in the New Testament, by precept nor by example.* In these letters I have laid before you the testimony of many of these eminent men, proving, conclusively, that the baptism of infants is not authorized nor required in the New Testament Scriptures. And one of these witnesses, Rev. A. T. Bledsoe, D. D., LL. D., says: "With all our searching, we have been unable to find in the New Testament *a single express declaration or word in favor of infant baptism.*" He proposes, therefore, to "justify the

right *solely on the ground of logical inference*, and not on any express word of Christ or his apostles." And this, he assures us, is not "a singular opinion," adding: "Hundreds of learned pedobaptists have come to the same conclusion." There is not one argument for the baptism of infants in the whole range of pedobaptist literature that is not rejected as utterly worthless by multitudes of able and zealous pedobaptists, and universally the defenses set up by any one set of pedobaptists are repudiated and laughed at by hosts of others, equally intelligent and pious advocates of the same practice. This one undeniable fact is, of itself, a demonstration that infant baptism is not of God.

7. A multitude of the most eminent pedobaptist writers and scholars concede that the *Greek for baptism means immersion*.

In these letters I have placed before you a part only of the great host of such concessions made freely by the foremost scholars and thinkers of the entire pedobaptist world. No man can refute these concessions. Rarely, if ever, do we hear of one who has the hardihood to make the attempt. There is, indeed, a certain class of advocates of sprinkling who make reckless assertions about the meaning of the Greek term. I recollect a case in point. Some years ago, at the request of my brethren, I spoke on "Baptism" at one of my regular appointments, and showed, from pedobaptist authorities, that the word used by our Lord enjoining baptism means to immerse, arguing thence that the command to baptize is a command to immerse. A few days afterward, Rev. T. W——, a minister of the Methodist Episcopal Church, replied, admitting all I had said about the meaning of *baptizo* and its derivatives, but gravely assuring his hearers that neither *baptizo* nor its derivatives are ever used in the Scriptures to indicate baptism! I suppose the good brother did not know any better, and I trust his tribe is gradually dying out. But the fact remains, and daily grows more evident, that *real pedobaptist scholarship* condemns the pretensions of pedobaptist practices.

8. *Eminent pedobaptist expositors translate baptizo by immerse.* Such translation we have in Lange on Matthew, as you have already seen in these letters. And this is the only translation of the word that pedobaptist scholars dare to make, and it is to their credit that they do not attempt any other. Dean Stanley assures us that, "on philological grounds," such translation is correct. It is true, they might use some other word, such as *dip* or *plunge*—the equiva-

lent of *immerse*—but none others. Whenever the mass of our pedobaptist expositors undertake to translate *baptizo*, the occupation of the sprinklers will be gone. For one, I believe in the honesty and Christian integrity of our pedobaptist laity, and I am confident that when the time comes, as come it will, when they shall have before them the whole Bible honestly translated, they will arise in their might and utterly banish sprinkling from their churches. To-day they are befogged and misled by men from whom they have a right to expect better things; but to-morrow they will discover the deception, and their leaders will suddenly learn that it is "expedient" to translate the Word of God honestly and fully.

9. *The practice of restricted communion is scriptural and right, eminent pedobaptist writers and whole denominations of pedobaptists being judges.* It is true, that in these letters I have quoted only one pedobaptist writer on this subject, but his article is unanswerable. He vindicates the practice of the Presbyterian Church in restricting the privileges of the Lord's Table to those who, in the judgment of that Church, are duly baptized members of Evangelical Churches and properly qualified to partake of the sacred Supper. That vindication is complete. For

"Presbyterian Church" substitute "Baptist Churches," and it is none the less complete as a full vindication, a triumphant scriptural defense of our Baptist usage of restricted communion. In its application to practice among us, it cuts off Presbyterians from the Lord's Table, simply because, in the judgment of Baptist Churches, they are not scripturally baptized. Immersed members of pedobaptist churches are rejected from the Lord's Table by Baptists, because they "walk disorderly," living in avowed fellowship with erroneous doctrines and practices, and daily aiding and abetting usages and principles which, in their own baptism, they have condemned as unscriptural and wrong.

10. *The great contending forces, in this mighty conflict, are Christ and the world.* This is clearly shown by the testimony of Dean Stanley, quoted in my tenth letter. The change from immersion to sprinkling shows how "the spirit which lives and moves in human society can override even the most sacred ordinances." And the change from believers' baptism to infant baptism, conceded and traced out by this writer, and by many others, shows the same thing even more forcibly. Here are the facts: Christ establishes a sacred ordinance, gives it the sanc-

tion of his own example, and confirms it with all the weight and authority of a solemn, formal command. For a time it is duly observed by his professed people, but a change comes. "The spirit which lives and moves in human society" overrides it—changes its form, its subject, its significance, if not its entire substance—setting aside the example and authority of Christ in the house of his professed friends; and the whole Christian world, excepting only "the austere sect of the Baptists," follows this "*spirit* which lives and moves in human society." Only "the austere sect of the Baptists" refuses to bow down to this *spirit*. In the general stampede from Christ, they alone remain loyal to him; they alone cherish his most sacred ordinances; they alone recognize his command as the supreme rule of conduct.

The late Dean Stanley, one of the most eminent of pedobaptist authorities, being judge, the controversy is between Christ and the "austere sect of the Baptists," on one side, and "the spirit which lives and moves in human society" and the whole pedobaptist world, on the other side. This is substantially the latest pedobaptist statement of the case, and it certainly contains "food for thought." Though seemingly rash, it is undeniably true. The Baptists are contending for the "old paths," and for a full recognition of the authority of Christ in his own Church against those who prefer to do the bidding of "the spirit which lives and moves in human society," by overriding the most sacred ordinances. Alas! that the great majority of those who profess to be the friends of our Lord should be found in alliance with his most determined foe—"the spirit which lives and moves in human society."

I thank God, that in this conflict, so strange and unnatural, I am permitted to march and do battle under the banner of the Lord Jesus, with the few, rather than under the lead of that *spirit* which overrides the most sacred ordinances, with the many.

Now my dear brother, I think you can, in some good degree, understand how it is that I can not accept your courteous invitation to return to my old pedobaptist church home. Out of their own mouths, pedobaptists stand convicted of heretical, schismatic and unscriptural practices. By their own showing, they are engaged in overriding and perverting a sacred ordinance, instituted by our Lord himself, "teaching for doctrines the commandments of men," and substituting for ordinances the inventions of men. As a loyal disciple of the

Master, I can not fellowship these "unfruitful works of darkness." It is clearly my duty to "rather reprove them." And, in the light of the ever-growing evidence of their true character and tendencies, my disposition to "reprove them" coincides very fully with my duty. In fact, I think you may write me down a confirmed Baptist of the strictest sort. I can not be anything else and be loyal to the Word of God. Doubless we Baptists have much to learn—whole continents of truth, it may be—though I can not imagine what particular quarter of the spiritual universe such continents occupy; and we certainly have much to correct, and vast improvements to make in our daily walk, before we attain to perfection; but by grace we are what we are, and by grace we hope daily to approximate more nearly the true ideal of a Christian people. But we are not alone in our defects, though we do seem to be pretty much alone in our unswerving fealty to Christ. And this I say, not to boast of our obedience, but in a brotherly way, to rebuke the disobedience of others. And that disobedience is no "man of straw," set up as a pretext for battle, but a widespread, arrogant and persistent revolt against the authority of Christ, among those who call themselves his friends. The revolt of pedobaptism has long been a very lively and terrible thing. From its beginning it has ever been a persecutor of such of the Lord's people as would not tamely submit to its dictation. Thank God, the Inquisition is abolished, the fires of Smithfield are quenched, and the whipping-posts of Boston are a thing of the past. They no more terrify those who would observe the ordinances of the Lord's house in the way that the Master directs. But their existence and deadly work, and their origin, who can forget? They were called into existence by "the spirit that lives and moves in human society," to execute his bloody behests, that he might "override even the most sacred ordinances." And though they have been banished by an outraged and indignant humanity, in some greater degree enlightened by the spirit of the gospel, yet the "spirit" that contrived and employed them still lives, and still pursues with relentless purpose, but by different methods, his great scheme of opposing Christ and "overriding" his "most sacred ordinances." To-day he persecutes, wherever he can, by social forces, by parental authority and by churchly influences.

This is no idle fancy. Even now we have a most painful case of it in this city, directed against a member of my congregation, who desires to unite with my church. It is quite astonishing how our pedobaptist friends love us, until some of their friends show indications of becoming Baptists. I always did sympathize with the persecuted, and, in this class of cases, knowing them to be the better Christians, such unfairness as I too frequently witness only makes me love the Baptists the more.

But, my brother, what of the night with you? Will you still remain a pedobaptist, despite the burning rays of these FOOT-LIGHTS? Perhaps you may think there is some mistake about these testimonies. If so, please take your time and investigate them thoroughly. Examine the lexicons, look into the encyclopædias, trace up the quotations, one by one. Read Mosheim, Neander, Lange, Meyer, Geikie and Stanley, and all the rest, for yourself, and then refute them if you can. And if you attempt a refutation, do me the favor to send it to me, and (D. V.) I will read every line of it with the utmost care; and if you make good your refutation, I will come back to the pedobaptists at once. But if you can not make such refutation satisfactory to your own judgment and conscience, then lose no time in abandoning a a bad cause. May the Lord direct your mind and heart into the knowledge and love of the truth, and that very speedily, that your life and labors and entire influence may tell on the side of truth. Why should you not march under the banner of Christ, rather than cower under the tyranny of that "spirit that lives and moves in human society," and that finds nothing else quite so agreeable as to "override even the most sacred ordinances" of the Lord's house, and to set at naught his divine authority? Does this way of putting it startle you? Rest assured, the question, in just that form, is fully warranted by the facts. I own that I am responsible for the question, but you are largely responsible for those facts that make it pertinent when addressed to you. Come, gird yourself, and tell me:

1. How you became a pedobaptist?
2. Why you remain a pedobaptist?
3. Whether you have ever thoroughly investigated pedobaptism in the light of God's Word, intent on learning the truth?
4. If so, whether you found infant baptism and sprinkling in the Bible?
5. If so, where you found them, chapter and verse?
6. If not, why do you continue to countenance them?
7. If not, why do you not utterly and speedily reject them?

A severe catechism? Well, not half as severe as the one the Master will put you through, by and by, if your pedobaptist practices really are not of God. Need I assure you that I seek only your good and the honor of the Master? I have no personal interest to promote in trying to open your eyes to the truth. Whether you become a Baptist, or remain a pedobaptist, is a matter of total indifference to all my personal interests. I have no ax to grind, not even a hatchet, but I do love the Master and his Church, and his truth, and I love my pedobaptist brethren so well that I dare to tell them the truth in hope of doing them good. My little catechism, consisting of only seven questions, will doubtless trouble you, but how then will you meet the inquisition of the Master when he comes forth to probe every thought of the heart? "Brethren, if our heart condemn us, God is greater than our heart and knoweth all things." Remember, my brother, that *truth only* is of real enduring value. The poet sings, as with prophetic ken:

>"Truth crushed to earth shall rise again ;
> The eternal years of God are hers ;
> But error, wounded, writhes in pain,
> And dies amid her worshipers."

In the hope that you will "buy the truth and sell it not," I have written you these letters. In my book "BEHIND THE SCENES," if you chance to read it, you will catch some glimpses of the struggle through which I passed in detecting and renouncing the errors of pedobaptism. At that time many of the pedobaptist testimonies quoted in these letters had not been written. Others were not within my reach. Only a few of them came to my knowledge at that time. But I read scores of pedobaptist defenses, subjecting each one to a friendly but rigid scrutiny, with ever-multiplying discoveries of their unsoundness and total inadequacy. Then, last of all, I read, searchingly and prayerfully, that Book of books, the Word of the living God, and was thoroughly convinced that sprinkling and infant baptism are not of God, and forthwith I gave them up. I will not say, "Go, thou, and do likewise," but rather, Go at once to the only safe rule of faith and practice—the Holy Scriptures—and search them daily for the right way. And if you find, as you surely will, that your pedobaptist practices are not taught in the Word of God, make haste to banish them from your creed and from your work. It is infinitely better to be right than to be popular at the expense of the truth. One man on the side of God is a majority. And though the multitude may array themselves against him for a time, yet God will approve, and ultimately the truth of God will prevail. As ever, yours,

F. M. IAMS.

BEHIND THE SCENES.

By REV. F. M. IAMS.

One of the most popular works ever published on "BAPTISM" and "COMMUNION."

In a series of sketches, for the most part narrating personal experiences, the author, formerly a Congregationalist, but now a Baptist minister, tells of the troubles experienced by pedobaptists in their efforts to sustain their own practices. At the same time, it shows the unsatisfactory and unavailing character of the arguments adduced; presenting those to establish the doctrines and practices of the Baptists, in such a manner that the reader is convinced before being aware of it, and wakes up to a sense of the duty of baptism and an "orderly walk."

The sketches were first published in the JOURNAL AND MESSENGER, of Cincinnati, O., and such was their popularity that thousands of copies were immediately sold to subscribers to that paper who had read the sketches as they appeared. The publisher is constantly receiving information of the conversion of one and another to Baptist views, by reading "BEHIND THE SCENES."

It is a duodecimo volume of 219 pages, on good paper, clear type, and well bound; and, in order that it may have THE WIDEST POSSIBLE CIRCULATION, the price has been put at ONLY 75 CENTS BY MAIL, POSTAGE PAID. Liberal reductions made to pastors and agents who promote the sale of the book. Agents wanted in every Baptist Church. Address

G. W. LASHER,

Publisher "Journal and Messenger,"

CINCINNATI, OHIO.

BEFORE THE FOOTLIGHTS.

By the Author of "BEHIND THE SCENES."

A SERIES OF LETTERS, in which the author, once a Congregational minister, but now a highly esteemed and successful Baptist pastor, replies to the inquiry of an old pedobaptist friend who asks: "WHY NOT RETURN TO YOUR OLD CHURCH HOME?"

In his answer the author tells his reasons, by reciting such facts and arguments as make the adherents of pedobaptism appear to be acting a part on the stage—"Before the Footlights"—while the writer looks on and criticises the performance, giving his reasons for not joining in the farce.

The style of the book is admirable; the arguments are ably and fairly presented, so that a child can understand them; the tone and spirit are kind, conciliatory and persuasive; but the facts and the quotations from various pedobaptist authors are so set forth, as to carry conviction to any but the most obdurate opponent.

The letters were first published in the JOURNAL AND MESSENGER; but the demand for their publication in a more permanent form has induced the author and the publisher to put them in the form of this well-printed and well-bound duodecimo volume of more than 220 pages, selling at the low price of only 75 cents, postage prepaid. Agents wanted in every church, to whom liberal discounts will be made. Send for terms. Address

G. W. LASHER,

Publisher "Journal and Messenger,"

CINCINNATI, O.

WHAT THE PAPERS SAY

OF

Behind the Scenes.

IF any of our readers want a book that, if read, will stiffen their backbone as Baptists, let them send to the JOURNAL AND MESSENGER, Cincinnati, O., and ask for "Behind the Scenes." We read the articles as they were printed in the columns of that paper, and pronounce them among the best things of the kind we ever read.—*Baptist Nation.*

WE have just received the book, and regard it as among the most interesting additions made to our literature on the baptismal question in half a dozen years. It will be interesting reading to Baptists and pedobaptists as well. We commend it heartily.—*Alabama Baptist.*

THE arguments are extremely telling and cogent, yet they are urged in a kind, Christian, not in the least bitter spirit. —*Christian Secretary.*

No one can fail to be benefited by reading carefully this unique book. Pedobaptists will find themselves fairly represented, and their views in general correctly stated.— *Texas Baptist.*

THE book has not a dull page in it, and is not only exceedingly interesting as a narrative, but can not but prove helpful to earnest, inquiring minds who desire to know and do their duty.—*Baptist Weekly.*

IT is not often that a book deserves to be read at once as this does by everybody, and especially by every pedobaptist. It tells the story of the baptismal controversy capitally. The little book will make an impression and rank first class in polemic literature.—*Herald of Truth.*

WE trust the book may accomplish great good in opening the eyes of our pedobaptist friends to the weakness and uncripturalness of their position, and that they may have not only light to see, but grace to follow the light.—*National Baptist.*

THE story is a captivating one; is bestudded at every point with sparkling gems of truth, and is so presented as to disarm prejudice at the outset. We know of no book so valuable as a hand-book for Baptists to use with their pedobaptist friends. Send and get the book and loan it, and keep on loaning it.—*Am. Bap. Reflector.*

WE emphatically commend the book. Our brethren in the ministry of other denominations ought to read it.—*Watch-Tower.*

THE sketches are well written, very sensible and pointed, and show very conclusively the inconsistencies of pedobapists and the logical correctness of Baptist views, as well as their accordance with Scripture. The book is not only interesting but very instructive, and should be read by old and young.—*Kind Words.*

WE congratulate the author and thank the publisher, and commend the volume to all our readers. It is the very book to put into the hands of inquiring pedobaptists. Send and get it.—*Arkansas Evangelist.*

As we said a few weeks ago, it is a book that will do to buy, to read and to lend.—*Texas Baptist Herald.*

THESE sketches as they appeared in the JOURNAL AND MESSENGER attracted wide attention. In the permanent form in which they now appear, they are worthy of the widest circulation.—*Zion's Advocate.*

IT is the very book for the masses of the people and for Baptists to loan to their pedobaptist neighbors and relatives. —*Tennessee Baptist.*

THE book is not only interesting but very instructive, and should be read by old and young.—*Biblical Recorder.*

THE book ought to be in every Baptist family, and it is an excellent thing to put into the hands of any who desire to know about the Baptists. We give it hearty commendation.—*Central Baptist.*

NO recent contribution to Baptist literature has been more gladly welcomed.—*Mich. Christian Herald.*

WE are pained to know that Mr. Iams charges pedobaptists with lack of candor, but it is more painful to observe that he has proved his case.—*Watchman.*

We had one chapter of its contents in the MESSENGER a few weeks since, and may possibly extract another shortly, but the book should be read to be fully appreciated.—*Christian Messenger, Halifax, Nova Scotia.*

THERE is no dullness, nor sameness, nor weariness going over old ground, in a single page. It is bright, spicy, eloquent, amusing, instructive, with a frank, manly, Pauline piety and devotion to truth, which can not fail to profit every reader.

This book is so well and wittily written that it would interest a man who cared nothing for Christ's commands. It is, of all books on the subject we have seen, the best for Baptists to put into the hands of pedobaptist friends; the New Testament, of course, excepted. It is the very thing for the young Baptists to read on this subject, and it will be a treat to older Baptists who have grown a little weary of the usual style of such books.—*Western Recorder.*

Lightning Source UK Ltd.
Milton Keynes UK
UKHW022010071218
333658UK00009B/440/P